2008

to:

Wendell Joseph

from:

Professor Demsky

God loves you
personally - so
much - Always
trust Him

Promises for You from the New International Version
© 2004 by The Zondervan Corporation.
ISBN-10: 0-310-60470-2
ISBN-13: 978-0-310-60470-9
Previously published as *God's Promises for You from the New International Version*.

Developed and produced by The Livingstone Corporation. Project staff include: James
C. Galvin, Christopher D. Hudson, Lindsay Vanker, Thomas Ristow, and Kathleen
Ristow.

Requests for information should be addressed to:
Inspirio, the gift group of Zondervan
Grand Rapids, Michigan 49530
http://www.inspiriogifts.com

Cover and Interior design: Brand Navigation, LLC — DeAnna Pierce, Bill Chiaravalle,
www.brandnavigation.com
Cover photograph: ImageBank/Rob Atkins
Design Manager: Amy J. Wenger
Production Management: Matt Nolan
Editor: Tom Dean

Printed in China

06 07 08 /CTC/ 4 3 2 1

PROMISES *for* YOU

from the
NEW INTERNATIONAL
VERSION

inspirio™

TABLE of CONTENTS

PLAN *of* SALVATION

The Bible says that we have been separated and alienated from God because we have willfully turned our backs on Him and are determined to run our lives without Him. This is what the Bible means by sin—choosing our way instead of God's way, and not giving Him His rightful place in our lives. The evidence of this is all around us, in the moral chaos and heartache of our world. The headlines scream every day that we live in a broken, sin-ravaged world.

But in addition, the message declares that God still loves us. He yearns to forgive us and bring us back to Himself. He wants to fill our lives with meaning and purpose right now. Then He wants us to spend all eternity with Him in Heaven, free forever from the pain and sorrow and death of this world.

Moreover, God has done everything possible to reconcile us to Himself. He did this in a way that staggers our imagination. In God's plan, by His death on the Cross, Jesus Christ paid the penalty for our sins, taking the judgment of God that we deserve upon Himself when He died on the Cross. Now, by His resurrection from the dead, Christ has broken the bonds of death and opened the way to eternal life for us.

The resurrection also confirms for all time that Jesus was in fact who He said He was: the unique Son of God, sent from Heaven to save us from our sins. Now God freely offers us the gift of forgiveness and eternal life.

Finally, this message is about our response. Like any other gift, God's gift of salvation does not become ours until we accept it and make it our own. God has done everything possible to provide salvation. But we must reach out in faith and accept it.

How do we do this?

First, by confessing to God that we are sinners and in need of His forgiveness; by repenting off our sins and, with God's help, turning from them.

Second, by committing our lives to Jesus Christ as Lord and Savior. The best-known passage in the New Testament states the Gospel concisely: "For God so loved the world that he gave his one and only Son, that whoever believes in him shall not perish but have eternal life. For God did not send his Son into the world to condemn the world, but to save the world through him" (John 3:16–17). God in His grace invites us to receive His Son into our lives today.

If you have never done so, I invite you to bow your head right now, and by a simple prayer of faith, open your heart to Jesus Christ. God receives us just as we are. No matter who we are or what we have done, we are saved only because of what Christ has done for us. I will not go to Heaven because

I have preached to great crowds. I will go to Heaven for one reason: Jesus Christ died for me, and I am trusting Him alone for my salvation. Christ died for you also, and He freely offers you the gift of eternal life as you commit your life to Him.

When you do, you become a child of God, adopted into His family forever. He also comes to live within you and will begin to change you from within. No one who truly gives his or her life to Christ will ever be the same, for the promise of His Word is true: "Therefore, if anyone is in Christ, he is a new creation; the old has gone, the new has come! All this is from God, who reconciled us to himself through Christ and gave us the ministry of reconciliation" (2 Corinthians 5:17-18).

We have seen this happen countless times all over the world, and it can happen in your life as well. Open your life to Christ today.

ACCEPTANCE

JOHN 6:37

All that the Father gives me
will come to me,
and whoever comes to me
I will never drive away.

ROMANS 15:7

Accept one another, then,
just as Christ accepted you,
in order to bring praise to God.

1 TIMOTHY 4:9-10

This is a trustworthy saying
that deserves full acceptance
(and for this we labor and strive),
that we have put our hope in the living
God, who is the Savior of all men,
and especially of those who believe.

JAMES 2:2-4

Suppose a man comes into your meeting
wearing a gold ring and fine clothes,
and a poor man in shabby clothes also
comes in. If you show special attention
to the man wearing fine clothes and say,
"Here's a good seat for you,"
but say to the poor man, "You stand there"
or "Sit on the floor by my feet," have you
not discriminated among yourselves and
become judges with evil thoughts?

ROMANS 14:1

Accept him whose faith is weak,
without passing judgment
on disputable matters.

MATTHEW 7:2

For in the same way you judge others,
you will be judged,
and with the measure you use,
it will be measured to you.

ARMOR *of* GOD

2 CORINTHIANS 10:4

The weapons we fight with are not the
weapons of the world. On the contrary,
they have divine power to demolish
strongholds.

EPHESIANS 6:11

Put on the full armor of God so that you can
take your stand against the devil's
schemes.

ROMANS 13:12

The night is nearly over; the day is
almost here. So let us put aside the deeds
of darkness and put on the armor of light.

1 THESSALONIANS 5:8

But since we belong to the day, let us
be self-controlled, putting on faith and
love as a breastplate, and the hope of
salvation as a helmet.

EPHESIANS 6:17

Take the helmet of salvation and
the sword of the Spirit,
which is the word of God.

COLOSSIANS 3:12

As God's chosen people,
holy and dearly loved, clothe yourselves
with compassion, kindness, humility,
gentleness and patience.

HEBREWS 4:12

For the word of God is living and active.
Sharper than any double-edged sword,
it penetrates even to dividing
soul and spirit, joints and marrow;
it judges the thoughts and attitudes
of the heart.

1 PETER 5:5

Young men, in the same way
be submissive to those who are older.
All of you, clothe yourselves
with humility toward one another,
because, "God opposes the proud
but gives grace to the humble."

ASSURANCE

HEBREWS 11:1

Now faith is being sure of what we
hope for and certain of what we do not
see.

ROMANS 8:38-39

For I am convinced that neither death nor
life, neither angels nor demons, neither
the present nor the future, nor any powers, neither height nor depth, nor anything else in all creation, will be able to
separate us from the love of God that is
in Christ Jesus our Lord.

ISAIAH 54:10

"Though the mountains be shaken and
the hills be removed, yet my unfailing
love for you will not be shaken nor my
covenant of peace be removed," says the
LORD, who has compassion on you.

John 10:27-29

My sheep listen to my voice;
I know them, and they follow me.
I give them eternal life,
and they shall never perish;
no one can snatch them out of my hand.
My Father, who has given them to me,
is greater than all; no one can snatch
them out of my Father's hand.

2 Timothy 1:12

I am not ashamed, because I know whom
I have believed, and am convinced
that he is able to guard what I have
entrusted to him for that day.

1 John 5:14-15

This is the confidence we have
in approaching God:
that if we ask anything according
to his will, he hears us.
And if we know that he hears us—
whatever we ask—we know that
we have what we asked of him.

ATONEMENT

COLOSSIANS 1:19-20

For God was pleased to have all his
fullness dwell in him,
and through him to reconcile to himself
all things, whether things on earth
or things in heaven, by making peace
through his blood, shed on the cross.

COLOSSIANS 2:13-14

When you were dead in your sins and in
the uncircumcision of your sinful nature,
God made you alive with Christ.
He forgave us all our sins,
having canceled the written code,
with its regulations, that was against us
and that stood opposed to us;
he took it away, nailing it to the cross.

1 John 2:2

He is the atoning sacrifice
for our sins, and not only for ours
but also for the sins of the whole world.

1 Peter 1:18–19

For you know that it was not
with perishable things such as silver
or gold that you were redeemed
from the empty way of life handed down
to you from your forefathers,
but with the precious blood of Christ,
a lamb without blemish or defect.

Romans 5:9

Since we have now been justified
by his blood, how much more shall we be
saved from God's wrath through him!

Hebrews 9:28

Christ was sacrificed once
to take away the sins of many people;
and he will appear a second time,
not to bear sin, but to bring salvation
to those who are waiting for him.

BELIEF

JOHN 3:16

For God so loved the world
that he gave his one and only Son,
that whoever believes in him
shall not perish but have eternal life.

JOHN 6:47

I tell you the truth,
he who believes has everlasting life.

ROMANS 10:9-10

If you confess with your mouth,
"Jesus is Lord,"
and believe in your heart that
God raised him from the dead,
you will be saved.
For it is with your heart
that you believe and are justified,
and it is with your mouth
that you confess and are saved.

JOHN 11:25-26

Jesus said to her, "I am the resurrection
and the life. He who believes in me
will live, even though he dies;
and whoever lives and believes in me
will never die. Do you believe this?"

ACTS 16:31

They replied, "Believe in the Lord Jesus,
and you will be saved—
you and your household."

JOHN 3:18

Whoever believes in him is not condemned.

ACTS 10:43

All the prophets testify about him
that everyone who believes in him receives
forgiveness of sins through his name.

JOHN 20:29

Jesus told him,
"Because you have seen me,
you have believed;
blessed are those who have not seen
and yet have believed."

BLESSINGS

PSALM 1:1-2

Blessed is the man who does not walk
in the counsel of the wicked
or stand in the way of sinners
or sit in the seat of mockers.
But his delight is in
the law of the LORD, and on his law
he meditates day and night.

JEREMIAH 17:7

Blessed is the man
who trusts in the LORD,
whose confidence is in him.

EPHESIANS 1:3

Praise be to the God and Father
of our Lord Jesus Christ,
who has blessed us
in the heavenly realms with
every spiritual blessing in Christ.

Psalm 31:19

How great is your goodness, which you
have stored up for those who fear you,
which you bestow in the sight of men
on those who take refuge in you.

Psalm 103:2-3

Praise the LORD, O my soul,
and forget not all his benefits—
who forgives all your sins
and heals all your diseases.

Romans 10:12-13

For there is no difference
between Jew and Gentile—
the same Lord is Lord of all
and richly blesses all who call on him,
for, "Everyone who calls
on the name of the Lord will be saved."

James 1:17

Every good and perfect gift is from
above, coming down from the Father of
the heavenly lights, who does not
change like shifting shadows.

PSALM 16:11

You have made known to me the path of life;
you will fill me with joy in your presence,
with eternal pleasures at your right hand.

PSALM 65:4

Blessed are those you choose
and bring near to live in your courts!
We are filled with the good things
of your house, of your holy temple.

EZEKIEL 34:26-27

I will bless them and
the places surrounding my hill.
I will send down showers in season;
there will be showers of blessing.
The trees of the field will yield their
fruit and the ground will yield its crops;
the people will be secure in their land.
They will know that I am the LORD,
when I break the bars of their yoke
and rescue them from the hands
of those who enslaved them.

JOHN 1:16

From the fullness of his grace we have all
received one blessing after another.

MALACHI 3:10

"Bring the whole tithe into the storehouse,
that there may be food in my house.
Test me in this," says the LORD Almighty,
"and see if I will not throw open the
floodgates of heaven and pour out
so much blessing that you
will not have room enough for it."

DEUTERONOMY 11:26–27

See, I am setting before you today
a blessing and a curse—the blessing
if you obey the commands of the LORD
your God that I am giving you today.

GENESIS 12:2–3

I will make you into a great nation
and I will bless you;
I will make your name great,
and you will be a blessing.
I will bless those who bless you,
and whoever curses you I will curse;
and all peoples on earth
will be blessed through you.

BOLDNESS

HEBREWS 10:23
Let us hold unswervingly
to the hope we profess,
for he who promised is faithful.

ROMANS 1:16
I am not ashamed of the gospel,
because it is the power of God for the
salvation of everyone who believes:
first for the Jew, then for the Gentile.

PHILIPPIANS 1:20
I eagerly expect and hope that
I will in no way be ashamed, but will
have sufficient courage so that now
as always Christ will be exalted in my
body, whether by life or by death.

ISAIAH 40:29
He gives strength to the weary
and increases the power of the weak.

2 TIMOTHY 1:12

I am not ashamed, because I know whom
I have believed, and am convinced that
he is able to guard what I have
entrusted to him for that day.

PSALM 27:1

The LORD is my light and my salvation—
whom shall I fear? The LORD is the
stronghold of my life—of whom shall I
be afraid?

ROMANS 8:31-32

If God is for us, who can be against us?
He who did not spare his own Son,
but gave him up for us all—
how will he not also, along with him,
graciously give us all things?

DEUTERONOMY 31:6

Be strong and courageous. Do not be
afraid or terrified because of them,
for the LORD your God goes with you;
he will never leave you nor forsake you.

CELEBRATION

ISAIAH 61:10

I delight greatly in the LORD;
my soul rejoices in my God.
For he has clothed me with garments of
salvation and arrayed me in a robe of
righteousness, as a bridegroom adorns
his head like a priest, and as a bride
adorns herself with her jewels.

PSALM 30:11-12

You turned my wailing into dancing;
you removed my sackcloth
and clothed me with joy,
that my heart may sing to you
and not be silent. O LORD my God,
I will give you thanks forever.

PSALM 149:3

Let them praise his name with dancing
and make music to him
with tambourine and harp.

Isaiah 12:6

Shout aloud and sing for joy,
people of Zion, for great
is the Holy One of Israel among you.

Zephaniah 3:17

The LORD your God is with you,
he is mighty to save.
He will take great delight in you,
he will quiet you with his love,
he will rejoice over you with singing.

Exodus 15:2

The LORD is my strength and my song;
he has become my salvation.
He is my God, and I will praise him,
my father's God, and I will exalt him.

Psalm 47:1-2

Clap your hands, all you nations;
shout to God with cries of joy.
How awesome is the LORD Most High,
the great king over all the earth!

CHARACTER

JAMES 3:13

Who is wise and understanding
among you? Let him show it
by his good life, by deeds done in
the humility that comes from wisdom.

1 TIMOTHY 4:12

Set an example for the believers in speech,
in life, in love, in faith and in purity.

ROMANS 12:17

Be careful to do what is right
in the eyes of everybody.

2 CORINTHIANS 1:12

Now this is our boast:
Our conscience testifies that we have
conducted ourselves in the world, and
especially in our relations with you, in the
holiness and sincerity that are from God.
We have done so not according to worldly
wisdom but according to God's grace.

PROVERBS 13:6

Righteousness guards the man of integrity,
but wickedness overthrows the sinner.

PSALM 84:11

For the LORD God is a sun and shield;
the LORD bestows favor and honor;
no good thing does he withhold
from those whose walk is blameless.

TITUS 3:1

Remind the people to be subject to
rulers and authorities, to be obedient,
to be ready to do whatever is good.

JOB 17:9

The righteous will hold to their ways,
and those with clean hands
will grow stronger.

LUKE 16:10

Whoever can be trusted with very little
can also be trusted with much,
and whoever is dishonest with very little
will also be dishonest with much.

CHARITY

PROVERBS 14:21
Blessed is he who is kind to the needy.

MATTHEW 25:40
The king will reply, "I tell you the truth,
whatever you did for one of the least of
these brothers of mine, you did for me."

PROVERBS 22:9
A generous man will himself be blessed,
for he shares his food with the poor.

PROVERBS 28:27
He who gives to the poor will lack nothing,
but he who closes his eyes to them
receives many curses.

PROVERBS 19:17
He who is kind to the poor
lends to the Lord, and he will reward
him for what he has done.

PROVERBS 11:25

A generous man will prosper;
he who refreshes others
will himself be refreshed.

MATTHEW 10:42

If anyone gives even a cup of cold
water to one of these little ones
because he is my disciple,
I tell you the truth, he will certainly
not lose his reward.

LUKE 14:13–14

When you give a banquet,
invite the poor, the crippled, the lame,
the blind, and you will be blessed.
Although they cannot repay you,
you will be repaid at the resurrection
of the righteous.

2 CORINTHIANS 9:7

Each man should give what he has
decided in his heart to give,
not reluctantly or under compulsion,
for God loves a cheerful giver.

CHILDREN

PSALM 127:3-5

Sons are a heritage from the LORD,
children a reward from him.
Like arrows in the hands of a warrior
are sons born in one's youth.
Blessed is the man
whose quiver is full of them.

PROVERBS 22:6

Train a child in the way he should go,
and when he is old he will not turn from it.

PROVERBS 29:17

Discipline your son,
and he will give you peace;
he will bring delight to your soul.

PROVERBS 20:11

Even a child is known by his actions,
by whether his conduct is pure and right.

3 JOHN 1:4

I have no greater joy than to hear
that my children are walking in the truth.

PSALM 22:10

From birth I was cast upon you;
from my mother's womb
you have been my god.

PSALM 71:6

From birth I have relied on you;
you brought me forth from my
mother's womb. I will ever praise you.

PSALM 139:14–16

I praise you because I am fearfully and
wonderfully made;
your works are wonderful,
I know that full well.
My frame was not hidden from you
when I was made in the secret place.
When I was woven together in the
depths of the earth,
your eyes saw my unformed body.
All the days ordained for me
were written in your book
before one of them came to be.

DEUTERONOMY 11:18-21

Fix these words of mine
in your hearts and minds;
tie them as symbols on your hands
and bind them on your foreheads.
Teach them to your children, talking
about them when you sit at home
and when you walk along the road,
when you lie down and when you get up.
Write them on the doorframes
of your houses and on your gates,
so that your days and the days of your
children may be many in the land that
the LORD swore to give your forefathers,
as many as the days that
the heavens are above the earth.

PSALM 139:13

For you created my inmost being;
you knit me together
in my mother's womb.

MATTHEW 18:4

Whoever humbles himself like this child
is the greatest in the kingdom of heaven.

MARK 10:15

I tell you the truth, anyone who will
not receive the kingdom of God
like a little child will never enter it.

PSALM 78:5-7

He decreed statutes for Jacob
and established the law in Israel,
which he commanded our forefathers
to teach their children,
so the next generation would know them,
even the children yet to be born,
and they in turn would tell their children.
Then they would put their trust in God
and would not forget his deeds
but would keep his commands.

ACTS 2:38-39

Peter replied, "Repent and be baptized,
every one of you, in the name of Jesus
Christ for the forgiveness of your sins.
And you will receive the gift
of the Holy Spirit. The promise is for
you and your children and for all
who are far off—for all whom
the Lord our God will call."

CHILDREN *of* GOD

JOHN 1:12-13

Yet to all who received him,
to those who believed in his name,
he gave the right to become children
of God—children born not of natural
descent, nor of human decision
or a husband's will, but born of God.

ROMANS 8:16

The Spirit himself testifies with our
spirit that we are God's children.

ROMANS 8:14-15

Those who are led by the Spirit of God are
sons of God. For you did not receive a
spirit that makes you a slave again to fear,
but you received the Spirit of sonship.
And by him we cry, "Abba, Father."

2 CORINTHIANS 6:18

"I will be a Father to you,
and you will be my sons and daughters,"
says the Lord Almighty.

GALATIANS 4:6-7

Because you are sons,
God sent the Spirit of his Son into
our hearts, the Spirit who calls out,
"Abba, Father." So you are no longer
a slave, but a son; and since you are
a son, God has made you also an heir.

1 JOHN 3:1

How great is the love the Father has
lavished on us, that we should
be called children of God!
And that is what we are!
The reason the world does not know us
is that it did not know him.

1 JOHN 3:2

Dear friends, now we are children
of God, and what we will be has not yet
been made known. But we know that
when he appears, we shall be like him,
for we shall see him as he is.

CHILDREN'S DUTIES

DEUTERONOMY 5:16

Honor your father and your mother, as
the LORD your God has commanded you,
so that you may live long
and that it may go well with you in
the land the LORD your God is giving you.

PROVERBS 6:20-22

My son, keep your father's commands
and do not forsake your mother's teaching.
Bind them upon your heart forever;
fasten them around your neck.
When you walk, they will guide you;
when you sleep, they will watch over you;
when you awake, they will speak to you.

PROVERBS 8:32-33

Now then, my sons, listen to me;
blessed are those who keep my ways.
Listen to my instruction and be wise;
do not ignore it.

EPHESIANS 6:2

"Honor your father and mother"—which
is the first commandment with a promise.

PROVERBS 23:22

Listen to your father, who gave you life,
and do not despise your mother
when she is old.

PSALM 119:9

How can a young man keep his way pure?
By living according to your word.

PROVERBS 23:25

May your father and mother be glad;
may she who gave you birth rejoice!

1 TIMOTHY 5:4

If a widow has children
or grandchildren, these should learn
first of all to put their religion
into practice by caring
for their own family and so repaying
their parents and grandparents,
for this is pleasing to God.

CHRIST'S RETURN

HEBREWS 9:28

So Christ was sacrificed once
to take away the sins of many people;
and he will appear a second time,
not to bear sin, but to bring salvation
to those who are waiting for him.

ACTS 1:11

"Men of Galilee," they said, "why do
you stand here looking into the sky?
This same Jesus, who has been taken
from you into heaven,
will come back in the same way you
have seen him go into heaven."

REVELATION 1:7

Look, he is coming with the clouds,
and every eye will see him.

1 Thessalonians 4:16

For the Lord himself will come down
from heaven, with a loud command,
with the voice of the archangel
and with the trumpet call of God,
and the dead in Christ will rise first.

Revelation 22:12

Behold, I am coming soon!
My reward is with me, and I will give to
everyone according to what he has done.

2 Peter 3:10

The day of the Lord will come like a thief.
The heavens will disappear with a roar;
the elements will be destroyed by fire,
and the earth and everything in it
will be laid bare.

Luke 12:40

You also must be ready,
because the Son of Man will come
at an hour when you do not expect him.

CHURCH

1 PETER 2:9

You are a chosen people, a royal
priesthood, a holy nation, a people
belonging to God, that you may declare
the praises of him who called you
out of darkness into his wonderful light.

1 CORINTHIANS 12:27-28

Now you are the body of Christ, and
each one of you is a part of it.
And in the church God has appointed
first of all apostles, second prophets,
third teachers, then workers of miracles,
also those having gifts of healing,
those able to help others, those with
gifts of administration, and those
speaking in different kinds of tongues.

1 CORINTHIANS 12:12-13

The body is a unit, though it is made
up of many parts; and though all its
parts are many, they form one body. So
it is with Christ. For we were all
baptized by one Spirit into one body—
whether Jews or Greeks, slave or
free—and we were all given the one
Spirit to drink.

COLOSSIANS 1:18

He is the head of the body, the church; he
is the beginning and the firstborn from
among the dead, so that in everything he
might have the supremacy.

ROMANS 12:4-6

Just as each of us has one body with many
members, and these members do not all
have the same function, so in Christ we
who are many form one body, and each
member belongs to all the others.
We have different gifts,
according to the grace given us.
If a man's gift is prophesying,
let him use it in proportion to his faith.

1 TIMOTHY 3:15
God's household … is the church
of the living God,
the pillar and foundation of the truth.

EPHESIANS 4:11–13
It was he who gave some to be apostles,
some to be prophets, some to be
evangelists, and some to be pastors and
teachers, to prepare God's people
for works of service, so that
the body of Christ may be built up
until we all reach unity in the faith
and in the knowledge of the Son of God
and become mature, attaining to the whole
measure of the fullness of Christ.

HEBREWS 13:17
Obey your leaders and submit to
their authority. They keep watch over you
as men who must give an account.
Obey them so that their work
will be a joy, not a burden,
for that would be of no advantage to you.

COLOSSIANS 3:16

Let the word of Christ dwell in you richly
as you teach and admonish one another
with all wisdom, and as you sing psalms,
hymns and spiritual songs with gratitude
in your hearts to God.

ACTS 2:42-47

They devoted themselves to the apostles'
teaching and to the fellowship,
to the breaking of bread and to prayer.
Everyone was filled with awe,
and many wonders and miraculous signs
were done by the apostles.
All the believers were together
and had everything in common.
Selling their possessions and goods,
they gave to anyone as he had need.
Every day they continued to meet together
in the temple courts. They broke bread
in their homes and ate together
with glad and sincere hearts,
praising God and enjoying the favor of all
the people. And the Lord added to their
number daily those who were being saved.

COMFORT

2 CORINTHIANS 1:3-4

Praise be to the God and Father of our
LORD Jesus Christ, the Father of
compassion and the God of all comfort,
who comforts us in all our troubles, so
that we can comfort those in any
trouble with the comfort we ourselves
have received from God.

PSALM 34:18

The LORD is close to the brokenhearted
and saves those who are crushed in spirit.

REVELATION 7:17

For the Lamb at the center of the throne
will be their shepherd;
he will lead them to springs of living
water.
And God will wipe away every tear
from their eyes.

ISAIAH 66:13

As a mother comforts her child,
so will I comfort you;
and you will be comforted over Jerusalem.

DEUTERONOMY 33:12

Let the beloved of the Lord
rest secure in him, for he shields him
all day long and the one the Lord loves
rests between his shoulders.

ISAIAH 57:18-19

"I have seen his ways,
but I will heal him;
I will guide him and restore comfort
to him, creating praise on the lips
of the mourners in Israel.
Peace, peace, to those far and near,"
says the LORD. "And I will heal them."

JEREMIAH 31:13

Then maidens will dance and be glad,
young men and old as well.
I will turn their mourning into gladness;
I will give them comfort and joy
instead of sorrow.

COMMITMENT

PSALM 37:5
Commit your way to the LORD;
trust in him and he will do this.

PROVERBS 16:3
Commit to the LORD whatever you do,
and your plans will succeed.

2 CHRONICLES 16:9
For the eyes of the LORD range
throughout the earth to strengthen those
whose hearts are fully committed to him.

PSALM 103:17-18
From everlasting to everlasting
the LORD's love is with those who
fear him, and his righteousness
with their children's children—
with those who keep his covenant
and remember to obey his precepts.

1 Kings 8:61

Your hearts must be fully committed to the LORD our God, to live by his decrees and obey his commands, as at this time.

Psalm 132:12

If your sons keep my covenant and the statutes I teach them, then their sons will sit on your throne for ever and ever.

Numbers 30:2

When a man makes a vow to the LORD or takes an oath to obligate himself by a pledge, he must not break his word but must do everything he said.

Deuteronomy 23:21

If you make a vow to the LORD your God, do not be slow to pay it, for the LORD your God will certainly demand it of you and you will be guilty of sin.

Ecclesiastes 5:4

When you make a vow to God, do not delay in fulfilling it. He has no pleasure in fools; fulfill your vow.

COMPASSION

NEHEMIAH 9:17
You are a forgiving God, gracious and
compassionate, slow to anger and
abounding in love.

PSALM 145:9
The LORD is good to all;
he has compassion on all he has made.

ISAIAH 30:18
Yet the LORD longs to be gracious to you;
he rises to show you compassion.
For the LORD is a God of justice.
Blessed are all who wait for him!

ISAIAH 54:10
"Though the mountains be shaken
and the hills be removed, yet my
unfailing love for you will not be shaken
nor my covenant of peace be removed,"
says the LORD, who has compassion on you.

Psalm 103:13

As a father has compassion on his children,
so the LORD has compassion on those
who fear him.

Hosea 2:19

I will betroth you to me forever;
I will betroth you in righteousness
and justice, in love and compassion.

Psalm 119:156

Your compassion is great, O LORD;
preserve my life according to your laws.

Lamentations 3:22-23

Because of the LORD's great love
we are not consumed,
for his compassions never fail.
They are new every morning;
great is your faithfulness.

2 Corinthians 1:3

Praise be to the God and Father
of our Lord Jesus Christ, the Father
of compassion and the God of all comfort.

CONFIDENCE

PROVERBS 3:26

For the LORD will be your confidence and
will keep your foot from being snared.

HEBREWS 13:6

We say with confidence,
"The Lord is my helper;
I will not be afraid.
What can man do to me?"

PSALM 27:3

Though an army besiege me,
my heart will not fear;
though war break out against me,
even then will I be confident.

HEBREWS 4:16

Let us then approach the throne of
grace with confidence, so that we may
receive mercy and find grace to help us
in our time of need.

PSALM 23:4
Even though I walk
through the valley of the shadow of death,
I will fear no evil, for you are with me;
your rod and your staff,
they comfort me.

1 JOHN 4:16-17
We know and rely on the love
God has for us. God is love.
Whoever lives in love lives in God,
and God in him.
In this way, love is made complete
among us so that we will have
confidence on the day of judgment,
because in this world we are like him.

1 JOHN 5:14
This is the confidence we have in
approaching God: that if we ask anything
according to his will, he hears us.

1 JOHN 2:28
Now, dear children, continue in him, so
that when he appears we may be confident
and unashamed before him at his coming.

CONSOLATION

Psalm 147:3

He heals the brokenhearted and
binds up their wounds.

Psalm 34:18

The LORD is close
to the brokenhearted
and saves those
who are crushed in spirit.

Revelation 14:13

Then I heard a voice from heaven say,
"Write: Blessed are the dead who
die in the Lord from now on."
"Yes," says the Spirit,
"they will rest from their labor,
for their deeds will follow them."

Psalm 116:15

Precious in the sight of the LORD
is the death of his saints.

PHILIPPIANS 1:21

For to me, to live is Christ
and to die is gain.

ROMANS 14:8

If we live, we live to the Lord;
and if we die, we die to the Lord.
So, whether we live or die,
we belong to the Lord.

2 CORINTHIANS 5:8

We are confident, I say, and would
prefer to be away from the body
and at home with the Lord.

2 CORINTHIANS 1:3-4

Praise be to the God and Father
of our Lord Jesus Christ,
the Father of compassion and
the God of all comfort,
who comforts us in all our troubles,
so that we can comfort those
in any trouble with the comfort
we ourselves have received from God.

CONTENTMENT

PHILIPPIANS 4:11–12

I am not saying this because I am in need,
for I have learned to be content
whatever the circumstances.
I know what it is to be in need,
and I know what it is to have plenty.
I have learned the secret of being content
in any and every situation,
whether well fed or hungry,
whether living in plenty or in want.

PROVERBS 19:23

The fear of the LORD leads to life:
Then one rests content, untouched by trouble.

1 TIMOTHY 6:6

Godliness with contentment is great gain.

HEBREWS 13:5

Keep your lives free from the love of money and be content with what you have, because God has said, "Never will I leave you; never will I forsake you."

JOB 1:21

Naked I came from my mother's womb, and naked I will depart.
The LORD gave and the LORD has taken away;
may the name of the LORD be praised.

1 TIMOTHY 6:8

If we have food and clothing, we will be content with that.

PSALM 16:2

I said to the LORD, "You are my LORD; apart from you I have no good thing."

PROVERBS 15:15

The cheerful heart has a continual feast.

COURAGE

PSALM 31:24

Be strong and take heart,
all you who hope in the LORD.

PSALM 27:14

Wait for the LORD;
be strong and take heart
and wait for the LORD.

ISAIAH 43:2-3

When you pass through the waters,
I will be with you;
and when you pass through the rivers,
they will not sweep over you.
When you walk through the fire,
you will not be burned;
the flames will not set you ablaze.
For I am the LORD, your God,
the Holy One of Israel, your Savior.

Psalm 28:7

The LORD is my strength and my shield;
my heart trusts in him, and I am helped.
My heart leaps for joy
and I will give thanks to him in song.

Deuteronomy 7:21

The LORD your God, who is among you,
is a great and awesome God.

Isaiah 41:10

I will strengthen you and help you;
I will uphold you with
my righteous right hand.

Psalm 18:32

It is God who arms me with strength
and makes my way perfect.

Isaiah 40:29

He gives strength to the weary
and increases the power of the weak.

Psalm 18:29

With your help I can advance
against a troop;
with my God I can scale a wall.

DAILY WALK

DEUTERONOMY 5:33

Walk in all the way that the LORD
your God has commanded you, so that you
may live and prosper and prolong your
days in the land that you will possess.

PROVERBS 4:25–26

Let your eyes look straight ahead,
fix your gaze directly before you.
Make level paths for your feet
and take only ways that are firm.

1 TIMOTHY 6:11–12

Flee from all this, and pursue
righteousness, godliness, faith, love,
endurance and gentleness. Fight the good
fight of the faith. Take hold of the eternal life to which you were called when
you made your good confession in
the presence of many witnesses.

Galatians 5:25

Since we live by the Spirit,
let us keep in step with the Spirit.

Colossians 3:23

Whatever you do, work at it with all your
heart, as working for the Lord, not for
men.

1 Thessalonians 4:1

Finally, brothers, we instructed you
how to live in order to please God,
as in fact you are living.
Now we ask you and urge you in the
Lord Jesus to do this more and more.

Colossians 1:10

We pray this in order that you may live
a life worthy of the Lord and may
please him in every way:
bearing fruit in every good work,
growing in the knowledge of God.

Ephesians 5:15

Be very careful, then, how you live—
not as unwise but as wise.

DECISIONS

JEREMIAH 6:16
This is what the LORD says:
"Stand at the crossroads and look;
ask for the ancient paths,
ask where the good way is, and walk in it,
and you will find rest for your souls."

JAMES 1:5
If any of you lacks wisdom, he should ask
God, who gives generously to all without
finding fault, and it will be given to him.

JEREMIAH 33:3
Call to me and I will answer you
and tell you great and unsearchable
things you do not know.

PSALM 37:4
Delight yourself in the LORD
and he will give you
the desires of your heart.

John 14:16-17

I will ask the Father, and he will give
you another Counselor to be with you
forever—the Spirit of truth.
The world cannot accept him, because
it neither sees him nor knows him.
But you know him, for he lives with you
and will be in you.

Haggai 1:5

Now this is what the LORD Almighty
says: "Give careful thought to your ways."

Proverbs 3:5-6

Trust in the LORD with all your heart
and lean not on your own understanding;
in all your ways acknowledge him,
and he will make your paths straight.

Proverbs 16:9

In his heart a man plans his course,
but the LORD determines his steps.

Psalm 37:5

Commit your way to the LORD;
trust in him.

DELIVERANCE

2 SAMUEL 22:1

David sang to the LORD the words of
this song when the Lord delivered him
from the hand of all his enemies
and from the hand of Saul.

2 SAMUEL 22:2

He said:
"The LORD is my rock, my fortress
and my deliverer."

PSALM 34:17

The righteous cry out,
and the LORD hears them;
he delivers them from all their troubles.

PSALM 107:6

They cried out to the LORD in their trouble,
and he delivered them from their distress.

2 PETER 2:9

The Lord knows how to rescue godly
men from trials and to hold the
unrighteous for the day of judgment,
while continuing their punishment.

PSALM 34:7

The angel of the LORD encamps around
those who fear him, and he delivers them.

PSALM 32:7

You are my hiding place; you will
protect me from trouble and surround
me with songs of deliverance.

PSALM 116:8

For you, O LORD, have delivered my
soul from death, my eyes from tears,
my feet from stumbling.

PSALM 91:14-15

"Because he loves me," says the LORD,
"I will rescue him; I will protect him, for
he acknowledges my name. He will call
upon me, and I will answer him; I will be
with him in trouble, I will deliver him
and honor him."

DETERMINATION

ISAIAH 50:7

Because the Sovereign LORD helps me,
I will not be disgraced.
Therefore have I set my face like flint,
and I know I will not be put to shame.

1 CORINTHIANS 15:58

My dear brothers, stand firm.
Let nothing move you.
Always give yourselves fully to the work
of the Lord, because you know that your
labor in the Lord is not in vain.

REVELATION 3:11

I am coming soon. Hold on to what you
have, so that no one will take your crown.

GALATIANS 6:9

Let us not become weary in doing good,
for at the proper time we will
reap a harvest if we do not give up.

1 PETER 5:8-9

Be self-controlled and alert.
Your enemy the devil prowls around like a
roaring lion looking for someone to
devour. Resist him, standing firm in the
faith, because you know that your brothers throughout the world are undergoing
the same kind of sufferings.

DEUTERONOMY 4:9

Only be careful, and watch yourselves
closely so that you do not forget the
things your eyes have seen or let them
slip from your heart as long as you live.
Teach them to your children and to their
children after them.

PSALM 17:3

Though you probe my heart
and examine me at night,
though you test me, you will find nothing;
I have resolved that my mouth will not sin.

PSALM 119:11

I have hidden your word in my heart
that I might not sin against you.

DEVOTION

JOB 11:13, 15, 18

If you devote your heart to him
and stretch out your hands to him ...
then you will lift up your face
without shame; you will stand firm
and without fear. ...
You will be secure, because there is hope;
you will look about you
and take your rest in safety.

ACTS 2:41-43

Those who accepted his message
were baptized, and about three thousand
were added to their number that day.
They devoted themselves to the apostles'
teaching and to the fellowship,
to the breaking of bread and to prayer.
Everyone was filled with awe, and many
wonders and miraculous signs
were done by the apostles.

Psalm 141:8

My eyes are fixed on you,
O Sovereign LORD; in you I take refuge.

Deuteronomy 6:5

Love the LORD your God
with all your heart and with all your soul
and with all your strength.

Psalm 86:2

Guard my life, for I am devoted to you.
You are my God;
save your servant who trusts in you.

2 Chronicles 16:9

For the eyes of the LORD range
throughout the earth to strengthen
those whose hearts
are fully committed to him.

DISCERNMENT

JOHN 16:13

When he, the Spirit of truth, comes,
he will guide you into all truth.
He will not speak on his own;
he will speak only what he hears, and
he will tell you what is yet to come.

2 TIMOTHY 2:7

Reflect on what I am saying, for the
Lord will give you insight into all this.

JOHN 16:15

All that belongs to the Father is mine.
That is why I said the Spirit will take
from what is mine and make it known to you.

1 THESSALONIANS 5:21-22

Test everything. Hold on to the good.
Avoid every kind of evil.

1 JOHN 2:3

We know that we have come to know him
if we obey his commands.

1 Corinthians 2:14-16

The man without the Spirit does not
accept the things that come from the
Spirit of God, for they are foolishness
to him, and he cannot understand them,
because they are spiritually discerned.
The spiritual man makes judgments about
all things, but he himself is not subject
to any man's judgment:
"For who has known the mind of the Lord
that he may instruct him?"
But we have the mind of Christ.

1 John 4:6

We are from God, and whoever knows God
listens to us; but whoever is not from God
does not listen to us.
This is how we recognize the Spirit of
truth and the spirit of falsehood.

1 John 4:1

Test the spirits to see whether
they are from God, because many false
prophets have gone out into the world.

DISCIPLESHIP

JOHN 12:26

Whoever serves me must follow me; and where I am, my servant also will be. My Father will honor the one who serves me.

JOHN 10:27

My sheep listen to my voice; I know them, and they follow me.

JOHN 8:12

When Jesus spoke again to the people, he said, "I am the light of the world. Whoever follows me will never walk in darkness, but will have the light of life."

JOHN 14:21

Whoever has my commands and obeys them, he is the one who loves me. He who loves me will be loved by my Father, and I too will love him and show myself to him.

JOB 36:11

If they obey and serve him, they will spend the rest of their days in prosperity and their years in contentment.

JOHN 8:31

To the Jews who had believed him, Jesus said, "If you hold to my teaching, you are really my disciples."

JOHN 15:8

This is to my Father's glory, that you bear much fruit, showing yourselves to be my disciples.

JOHN 13:35

By this all men will know that you are my disciples, if you love one another.

2 TIMOTHY 4:1-2

In the presence of God and of Christ Jesus, who will judge the living and the dead, and in view of his appearing and his kingdom, I give you this charge: Preach the Word; be prepared in season and out of season; correct, rebuke and encourage—with great patience and careful instruction.

ELDERLY

TITUS 2:2-4

Teach the older men to be temperate,
worthy of respect, self-controlled, and
sound in faith, in love and in endurance.
Likewise, teach the older women to be
reverent in the way they live, not to be
slanderers or addicted to much wine,
but to teach what is good.
Then they can train the younger women
to love their husbands and children.

PROVERBS 16:31

Gray hair is a crown of splendor;
it is attained by a righteous life.

ISAIAH 46:4

Even to your old age and gray hairs
I am he,
I am he who will sustain you.
I have made you and I will carry you;
I will sustain you and I will rescue you.

Psalm 92:12-14

The righteous will flourish like a palm tree,
they will grow like a cedar of Lebanon;
planted in the house of the LORD,
they will flourish in the courts of our God.
They will still bear fruit in old age,
they will stay fresh and green.

Psalm 71:17-18

Since my youth, O God,
you have taught me, and to this day
I declare your marvelous deeds.
Even when I am old and gray,
do not forsake me, O God,
till I declare your power
to the next generation,
your might to all who are to come.

Psalm 37:25

I was young and now I am old, yet
I have never seen the righteous forsaken
or their children begging bread.

ENCOURAGEMENT

2 THESSALONIANS 2:16–17

May our Lord Jesus Christ himself
and God our Father, who loved us
and by his grace gave us eternal
encouragement and good hope,
encourage your hearts and strengthen
you in every good deed and word.

PSALM 10:17

You hear, O LORD, the desire
of the afflicted; you encourage them,
and you listen to their cry.

LAMENTATIONS 3:25–26

The LORD is good to those whose hope
is in him, to the one who seeks him;
it is good to wait quietly
for the salvation of the LORD.

JEREMIAH 29:11

"For I know the plans I have for you,"
declares the LORD, "plans to prosper
you and not to harm you,
plans to give you hope and a future."

LAMENTATIONS 3:21-23

This I call to mind
and therefore I have hope:
Because of the LORD's great love we
are not consumed,
for his compassions never fail.
They are new every morning;
great is your faithfulness.

PSALM 55:22

Cast your cares on the LORD
and he will sustain you;
he will never let the righteous fall.

1 THESSALONIANS 5:11

Encourage one another
and build each other up,
just as in fact you are doing.

ETERNAL LIFE

1 JOHN 2:17

The world and its desires pass away,
but the man who does the will of God
lives forever.

ROMANS 6:23

For the wages of sin is death,
but the gift of God is eternal life in
Christ Jesus our Lord.

JOHN 3:16

For God so loved the world that he gave
his one and only Son, that whoever
believes in him shall not perish
but have eternal life.

1 JOHN 5:11-12

This is the testimony: God has given us
eternal life, and this life is in his Son.
He who has the Son has life; he who does
not have the Son of God does not have life.

John 11:25-26

Jesus said to her, "I am the resurrection and the life. He who believes in me will live, even though he dies; and whoever lives and believes in me will never die."

John 3:36

Whoever believes in the Son has eternal life.

John 10:27-29

My sheep listen to my voice;
I know them, and they follow me.
I give them eternal life,
and they shall never perish;
no one can snatch them out of my hand. My
Father, who has given them to me,
is greater than all; no one can snatch them
out of my Father's hand.

John 17:3

Now this is eternal life:
that they may know you,
the only true God, and Jesus Christ,
whom you have sent.

EXPECTANCY

PSALM 37:7
Be still before the LORD
and wait patiently for him;
do not fret when men succeed in
their ways, when they carry out their
wicked schemes.

HOSEA 6:3
Let us acknowledge the LORD;
let us press on to acknowledge him.
As surely as the sun rises, he will appear;
he will come to us like the winter rains,
like the spring rains that water the earth.

PSALM 27:14
Wait for the LORD;
be strong and take heart
and wait for the LORD.

PSALM 130:5
I wait for the LORD, my soul waits,
and in his word I put my hope.

Psalm 40:1-2

I waited patiently for the LORD; he turned to me and heard my cry. He lifted me out of the slimy pit, out of the mud and mire; he set my feet on a rock and gave me a firm place to stand.

Isaiah 26:8

Yes, LORD, walking in the way of your laws, we wait for you; your name and renown are the desire of our hearts.

Micah 7:7

As for me, I watch in hope for the LORD, I wait for God my Savior; my God will hear me.

Isaiah 25:9

In that day they will say, "Surely this is our God; we trusted in him, and he saved us. This is the LORD, we trusted in him; let us rejoice and be glad in his salvation."

FAITH

HEBREWS 11:1

Now faith is being sure of what we hope
for and certain of what we do not see.

1 PETER 1:21

Through him you believe in God,
who raised him from the dead
and glorified him,
and so your faith and hope are in God.

1 PETER 1:8

Though you have not seen him,
you love him; and even though you
do not see him now, you believe in him
and are filled with an inexpressible
and glorious joy.

ROMANS 5:1

Since we have been justified through
faith, we have peace with God
through our Lord Jesus Christ.

1 Timothy 4:9–10

This is a trustworthy saying
that deserves full acceptance
(and for this we labor and strive),
that we have put our hope in the living
God, who is the Savior of all men,
and especially of those who believe.

John 14:12

I tell you the truth, anyone who has faith
in me will do what I have been doing.
He will do even greater things than these,
because I am going to the Father.

Matthew 17:20

I tell you the truth, if you have faith
as small as a mustard seed,
you can say to this mountain,
"Move from here to there"
and it will move.
Nothing will be impossible for you.

FAITHFULNESS

PROVERBS 3:3-4
Let love and faithfulness never leave you;
bind them around your neck,
write them on the tablet of your heart.
Then you will win favor and a good name
in the sight of God and man.

PSALM 31:23
Love the LORD, all his saints!
The LORD preserves the faithful,
but the proud he pays back in full.

2 SAMUEL 22:26
To the faithful
you show yourself faithful,
to the blameless
you show yourself blameless.

PSALM 37:28
For the LORD loves the just
and will not forsake his faithful ones.

PROVERBS 2:7-8

He holds victory in store for the upright,
he is a shield
to those whose walk is blameless,
for he guards the course of the just
and protects the way
of his faithful ones.

ISAIAH 26:3

You will keep in perfect peace
him whose mind is steadfast,
because he trusts in you.

REVELATION 2:10

Be faithful, even to the point of death,
and I will give you the crown of life.

REVELATION 13:10

If anyone is to go into captivity,
into captivity he will go.
If anyone is to be killed with the sword,
with the sword he will be killed.
This calls for patient endurance
and faithfulness on the part of the saints.

FAITHFULNESS *of* GOD

DEUTERONOMY 7:9

Know therefore that the LORD your God
is God; he is the faithful God,
keeping his covenant of love
to a thousand generations of those who
love him and keep his commands.

PSALM 100:5

For the LORD is good
and his love endures forever;
his faithfulness continues
through all generations.

ISAIAH 54:10

"Though the mountains be shaken
and the hills be removed,
yet my unfailing love for you
will not be shaken
nor my covenant of peace be removed,"
says the LORD,
who has compassion on you.

Psalm 111:7-8

The works of his hands
are faithful and just;
all his precepts are trustworthy.
They are steadfast for ever and ever,
done in faithfulness and uprightness.

1 Corinthians 1:9

God, who has called you into
fellowship with his Son Jesus Christ
our Lord, is faithful.

Psalm 18:25

To the faithful
you show yourself faithful.

1 John 1:9

If we confess our sins,
he is faithful and just
and will forgive us our sins and purify us
from all unrighteousness.

2 Thessalonians 3:3

The Lord is faithful,
and he will strengthen and protect you
from the evil one.

FAMILY

JOSHUA 24:15

Choose for yourselves this day
whom you will serve...
But as for me and my household,
we will serve the LORD.

GENESIS 18:19

For I have chosen him, so that he
will direct his children and his household
after him to keep the way of the LORD
by doing what is right and just.

PSALM 78:5-7

He decreed statutes for Jacob
and established the law in Israel,
which he commanded our forefathers
to teach their children,
so the next generation would know them,
even the children yet to be born,
and they in turn would tell their children.
Then they would put their trust in God
and would not forget his deeds
but would keep his commands.

Proverbs 31:15

She gets up while it is still dark;
she provides food for her family
and portions for her servant girls.

Isaiah 32:18

My people will live in peaceful
dwelling places, in secure homes,
in undisturbed places of rest.

Titus 2:3-5

Likewise, teach the older women
to be reverent in the way they live,
not to be slanderers or addicted
to much wine, but to teach what is good.
Then they can train the younger women to
love their husbands and children,
to be self-controlled and pure, to be busy
at home, to be kind, and to be subject to
their husbands, so that no one will malign
the word of God.

FELLOWSHIP

1 JOHN 4:12

No one has ever seen God; but if we love one another, God lives in us and his love is made complete in us.

JAMES 2:8

If you really keep the royal law found in Scripture, "Love your neighbor as yourself," you are doing right.

MATTHEW 5:44-45

I tell you: Love your enemies and pray for those who persecute you, that you may be sons of your Father in heaven.

1 PETER 4:8

Above all, love each other deeply, because love covers over a multitude of sins.

Luke 6:31

Do to others as you would have them do to you.

Philippians 2:3-4

In humility consider others better than yourselves. Each of you should look not only to your own interests, but also to the interests of others.

Colossians 3:12

As God's chosen people, holy and dearly loved, clothe yourselves with compassion, kindness, humility, gentleness and patience.

Romans 14:19

Let us therefore make every effort to do what leads to peace and to mutual edification.

Ephesians 4:29

Do not let any unwholesome talk come out of your mouths, but only what is helpful for building others up according to their needs, that it may benefit those who listen.

FINANCES

LUKE 12:15

He said to them, "Watch out!
Be on your guard against all kinds
of greed; a man's life does not consist
in the abundance of his possessions."

HEBREWS 13:5

Keep your lives free from the love
of money and be content
with what you have, because God has said,
"Never will I leave you;
never will I forsake you."

LUKE 16:10

Whoever can be trusted with very little
can also be trusted with much,
and whoever is dishonest with very little
will also be dishonest with much.

PROVERBS 3:9-10

Honor the LORD with your wealth,
with the firstfruits of all your crops;
then your barns will be filled
to overflowing, and your vats
will brim over with new wine.

MALACHI 3:10

"Bring the whole tithe into
the storehouse, that there may be food
in my house. Test me in this,"
says the LORD Almighty,
"and see if I will not throw open the
floodgates of heaven and pour out
so much blessing that you
will not have room enough for it."

2 CORINTHIANS 9:7

Each man should give what he has
decided in his heart to give,
not reluctantly or under compulsion,
for God loves a cheerful giver.

PROVERBS 28:27

He who gives to the poor will lack
nothing, but he who closes his eyes to
them receives many curses.

Luke 6:38

Give, and it will be given to you.
A good measure, pressed down, shaken
together and running over, will be poured
into your lap. For with the measure
you use, it will be measured to you.

Romans 13:8

Let no debt remain outstanding,
except the continuing debt to love one
another, for he who loves his fellowman
has fulfilled the law.

Proverbs 13:22

A good man leaves an inheritance
for his children's children,
but a sinner's wealth
is stored up for the righteous.

Deuteronomy 15:10

Give generously to him
and do so without a grudging heart;
then because of this the Lord your God
will bless you in all your work
and in everything you put your hand to.

MATTHEW 6:2-4

So when you give to the needy,
do not announce it with trumpets,
as the hypocrites do in the synagogues
and on the streets, to be honored by men.
I tell you the truth,
they have received their reward in full.
But when you give to the needy,
do not let your left hand know what
your right hand is doing,
so that your giving may be in secret.
Then your Father, who sees what is
done in secret, will reward you.

DEUTERONOMY 15:7-8

If there is a poor man among your
brothers in any of the towns of the
land that the LORD your God is giving
you, do not be hardhearted or tight-
fisted toward your poor brother.
Rather be openhanded
and freely lend him whatever he needs.

FORGIVENESS

EPHESIANS 4:32

Be kind and compassionate to one
another, forgiving each other,
just as in Christ God forgave you.

MATTHEW 6:14

For if you forgive men
when they sin against you, your heavenly
Father will also forgive you.

MATTHEW 18:21-22

Then Peter came to Jesus and asked,
"Lord, how many times
shall I forgive my brother
when he sins against me?
Up to seven times?" Jesus answered,
"I tell you, not seven times,
but seventy-seven times."

PROVERBS 10:12
Love covers over all wrongs.2

CORINTHIANS 2:10
If you forgive anyone, I also forgive him.
And what I have forgiven—if there was
anything to forgive—I have forgiven in
the sight of Christ for your sake.

LUKE 6:37
Forgive, and you will be forgiven.

MARK 11:25
When you stand praying, if you hold
anything against anyone, forgive him,
so that your Father in heaven may
forgive you your sins.

PROVERBS 17:9
He who covers over an offense
promotes love,
but whoever repeats the matter
separates close friends.

FORGIVENESS *of* GOD

Acts 2:38

Peter replied, "Repent and be baptized, every one of you, in the name of Jesus Christ for the forgiveness of your sins. And you will receive the gift of the Holy Spirit."

Romans 8:1-2

There is now no condemnation for those who are in Christ Jesus, because through Christ Jesus the law of the Spirit of life set me free from the law of sin and death.

Ephesians 1:7

In him we have redemption through his blood, the forgiveness of sins, in accordance with the riches of God's grace.

1 John 1:9

If we confess our sins, he is faithful and just and will forgive us our sins and purify us from all unrighteousness.

Colossians 2:13-14

When you were dead in your sins and in
the uncircumcision of your sinful nature,
God made you alive with Christ.
He forgave us all our sins,
having canceled the written code,
with its regulations, that was against us
and that stood opposed to us;
he took it away, nailing it to the cross.

Nehemiah 9:17

You are a forgiving God,
gracious and compassionate,
slow to anger and abounding in love.

Psalm 86:5

You are forgiving and good, O Lord,
abounding in love to all who call to you.

Isaiah 1:18

"Come now, let us reason together,"
says the LORD.
"Though your sins are like scarlet,
they shall be as white as snow;
though they are red as crimson,
they shall be like wool."

FREEDOM

ISAIAH 61:1

The Spirit of the Sovereign LORD is on me, because the LORD has anointed me to preach good news to the poor. He has sent me to bind up the brokenhearted, to proclaim freedom for the captives and release from darkness for the prisoners.

JOHN 8:32

You will know the truth, and the truth will set you free.

ROMANS 8:2

Through Christ Jesus the law of the Spirit of life set me free from the law of sin and death.

JOHN 8:36

If the Son sets you free, you will be free indeed.

2 Corinthians 3:17

Now the Lord is the Spirit, and where the Spirit of the Lord is, there is freedom.

Romans 6:22

Now that you have been set free from sin and have become slaves to God, the benefit you reap leads to holiness, and the result is eternal life.

Galatians 5:1

It is for freedom that Christ has set us free. Stand firm, then, and do not let yourselves be burdened again by a yoke of slavery.

Romans 7:6

Now, by dying to what once bound us, we have been released from the law so that we serve in the new way of the Spirit, and not in the old way of the written code.

Romans 8:21

The creation itself will be liberated from its bondage to decay and brought into the glorious freedom of the children of God.

FRESH START

Psalm 32:5

I acknowledged my sin to you
and did not cover up my iniquity.
I said, "I will confess
my transgressions to the LORD"—
and you forgave the guilt of my sin.

Isaiah 43:18–19

Forget the former things;
do not dwell on the past.
See, I am doing a new thing!
Now it springs up; do you not perceive it?
I am making a way in the desert
and streams in the wasteland.

Ezekiel 36:26

I will give you a new heart and put a new
spirit in you; I will remove from you
your heart of stone and give you a heart of
flesh.

Psalm 32:1-2

Blessed is he whose transgressions
are forgiven, whose sins are covered.
Blessed is the man whose sin the LORD
does not count against him and in
whose spirit is no deceit.

1 Peter 1:23

For you have been born again,
not of perishable seed,
but of imperishable, through
the living and enduring word of God.

Psalm 103:12

As far as the east is from the west,
so far has he removed
our transgressions from us.

1 Peter 1:3

Praise be to the God and Father of our
Lord Jesus Christ!
In his great mercy he has given us
new birth into a living hope
through the resurrection
of Jesus Christ from the dead.

FRIENDSHIP

PROVERBS 17:17
A friend loves at all times,
and a brother is born for adversity.

ROMANS 12:10
Be devoted to one another
in brotherly love.
Honor one another above yourselves.

JOHN 15:13
Greater love has no one than this,
that he lay down his life for his friends.

ECCLESIASTES 4:9–10
Two are better than one,
because they have a good return
for their work:
If one falls down,
his friend can help him up.
But pity the man who falls
and has no one to help him up!

Proverbs 18:24

A man of many companions
may come to ruin,
but there is a friend
who sticks closer than a brother.

Proverbs 13:20

He who walks with the wise
grows wise,
but a companion of fools
suffers harm.

Proverbs 27:17

As iron sharpens iron,
so one man sharpens another.

Proverbs 27:6

Wounds from a friend can be trusted,
but an enemy multiplies kisses.

Psalm 133:1

How good and pleasant it is
when brothers live together in unity!

FRIENDSHIP *of* GOD

REVELATION 3:20

Here I am! I stand at the door and knock.
If anyone hears my voice
and opens the door, I will come in
and eat with him, and he with me.

JOHN 14:23

Jesus replied, "If anyone loves me,
he will obey my teaching.
My Father will love him, and we will come
to him and make our home with him."

JAMES 2:23

The scripture was fulfilled that says,
"Abraham believed God, and it was
credited to him as righteousness,"
and he was called God's friend.

1 PETER 5:7

Cast all your anxiety on him
because he cares for you.

John 15:15

I no longer call you servants, because a servant does not know his master's business. Instead, I have called you friends, for everything that I learned from my Father I have made known to you.

1 Corinthians 1:9

God, who has called you into fellowship with his Son Jesus Christ our Lord, is faithful.

1 John 1:3

We proclaim to you what we have seen and heard, so that you also may have fellowship with us. And our fellowship is with the Father and with his Son, Jesus Christ.

Hosea 11:4

I led them with cords of human kindness, with ties of love; I lifted the yoke from their neck and bent down to feed them.

Jeremiah 15:15

You understand, O LORD; remember me and care for me.

FRUITFULNESS

EPHESIANS 5:9
The fruit of the light consists
in all goodness, righteousness and truth.

GALATIANS 5:22-23
The fruit of the Spirit is love, joy, peace,
patience, kindness, goodness,
faithfulness, gentleness and self-control.
Against such things there is no law.

JOHN 15:2
He cuts off every branch in me
that bears no fruit, while every branch
that does bear fruit he prunes
so that it will be even more fruitful.

JOHN 15:8
This is to my Father's glory,
that you bear much fruit,
showing yourselves to be my disciples.

JOHN 15:16

I chose you and appointed you to go
and bear fruit—fruit that will last.
Then the Father will give you whatever
you ask in my name.

MATTHEW 13:23

The one who received the seed that fell
on good soil is the man who hears the
word and understands it.
He produces a crop, yielding a hundred,
sixty or thirty times what was sown.

JOHN 12:24

I tell you the truth, unless a kernel
of wheat falls to the ground and dies,
it remains only a single seed.
But if it dies, it produces many seeds.

JOHN 15:5

I am the vine; you are the branches.
If a man remains in me and I in him,
he will bear much fruit;
apart from me you can do nothing.

MATTHEW 3:8

Produce fruit in keeping with repentance.

FUTURE

1 CORINTHIANS 2:9-10

As it is written: "No eye has seen,
no ear has heard, no mind has conceived
what God has prepared for those
who love him"—
but God has revealed it to us by his Spirit.
The Spirit searches all things,
even the deep things of God.

PHILIPPIANS 3:20-21

Our citizenship is in heaven.
And we eagerly await a Savior from there,
the Lord Jesus Christ, who,
by the power that enables him to bring
everything under his control,
will transform our lowly bodies so that
they will be like his glorious body.

1 John 3:2

Dear friends,
now we are children of God, and what we
will be has not yet been made known.
But we know that when he appears, we shall
be like him, for we shall see him as he is.

Jeremiah 29:11

"For I know the plans I have for you,"
declares the LORD, "plans to prosper
you and not to harm you, plans to give
you hope and a future."

Psalm 33:11

The plans of the LORD stand firm forever,
the purposes of his heart
through all generations.

Luke 12:37

It will be good for those servants whose
master finds them watching
when he comes. I tell you the truth,
he will dress himself to serve,
will have them recline at the table
and will come and wait on them.

GENEROSITY

LUKE 6:30

Give to everyone who asks you,
and if anyone takes what belongs to you,
do not demand it back.

2 CORINTHIANS 9:7

Each man should give what he has decided
in his heart to give, not reluctantly
or under compulsion,
for God loves a cheerful giver.

2 CORINTHIANS 9:6

Remember this: Whoever sows sparingly
will also reap sparingly, and whoever
sows generously will also reap
generously.

PSALM 112:5

Good will come to him who is generous
and lends freely, who conducts his
affairs with justice.

LUKE 6:38

Give, and it will be given to you.
A good measure, pressed down, shaken
together and running over, will be poured
into your lap. For with the measure
you use, it will be measured to you.

PROVERBS 22:9

A generous man will himself be blessed,
for he shares his food with the poor.

PSALM 37:25–26

I was young and now I am old,
yet I have never seen the righteous forsak-
en
or their children begging bread.
They are always generous and lend freely;
their children will be blessed.

1 TIMOTHY 6:18–19

Command them to do good,
to be rich in good deeds,
and to be generous and willing to share.
In this way they will lay up treasure for
themselves as a firm foundation
for the coming age, so that they may
take hold of the life that is truly life.

GENTLENESS

MATTHEW 11:29
Take my yoke upon you and learn from
me, for I am gentle and humble in heart,
and you will find rest for your souls.

COLOSSIANS 3:12
As God's chosen people,
holy and dearly loved, clothe yourselves
with compassion, kindness, humility,
gentleness and patience.

1 PETER 3:3-4
Your beauty...should be that
of your inner self, the unfading beauty
of a gentle and quiet spirit, which is of
great worth in God's sight.

1 TIMOTHY 6:11
You, man of God...
pursue righteousness, godliness,
faith, love, endurance and gentleness.

Ephesians 4:2

Be completely humble and gentle;
be patient, bearing with one another
in love.

Philippians 4:5

Let your gentleness be evident to all.
The Lord is near.

1 Peter 3:15

In your hearts set apart Christ as Lord.
Always be prepared to give an answer
to everyone who asks you to give
the reason for the hope that you have.
But do this with gentleness and respect.

Proverbs 15:1

A gentle answer turns away wrath.

Psalm 37:11

The meek will inherit the land
and enjoy great peace.

GIVING

2 CORINTHIANS 9:7

Each man should give what he has
decided in his heart to give, not
reluctantly or under compulsion, for
God loves a cheerful giver.

LUKE 6:38

Give, and it will be given to you. A good
measure, pressed down, shaken together
and running over, will be poured into
your lap. For with the measure you use, it
will be measured to you.

MALACHI 3:10

"Bring the whole tithe into the storehouse,
that there may be food in my house. Test
me in this," says the LORD Almighty, "and
see if I will not throw open the floodgates
of heaven and pour out so much blessing
that you will not have room enough for it."

ACTS 20:35

In everything I did, I showed you that by this kind of hard work we must help the weak, remembering the words the Lord Jesus himself said: "It is more blessed to give than to receive."

PROVERBS 25:21

If your enemy is hungry, give him food to eat; if he is thirsty, give him water to drink.

PROVERBS 28:27

He who gives to the poor will lack nothing, but he who closes his eyes to them receives many curses.

LUKE 6:30

Give to everyone who asks you, and if anyone takes what belongs to you, do not demand it back.

LUKE 11:13

If you then, though you are evil, know how to give good gifts to your children, how much more will your Father in heaven give the Holy Spirit to those who ask him!

GOALS

2 Corinthians 5:9

We make it our goal to please him,
whether we are at home in the body
or away from it.

Philippians 3:14

I press on toward the goal to win
the prize for which God has called me
heavenward in Christ Jesus.

Philippians 3:13-14

Brothers, I do not consider myself yet to
have taken hold of it.
But one thing I do: Forgetting what
is behind and straining toward what
is ahead, I press on toward the goal to win
the prize for which God has called me
heavenward in Christ Jesus.

2 TIMOTHY 2:15

Do your best to present yourself to God as
one approved, a workman who does not
need to be ashamed and who correctly
handles the word of truth.

1 CORINTHIANS 14:1

Follow the way of love and eagerly
desire spiritual gifts,
especially the gift of prophecy.

1 CORINTHIANS 12:31

Eagerly desire the greater gifts.

1 CORINTHIANS 9:24

Do you not know that in a race all the
runners run, but only one gets the prize?
Run in such a way as to get the prize.

1 CORINTHIANS 14:12

Since you are eager
to have spiritual gifts, try to excel in
gifts that build up the church.

1 THESSALONIANS 4:11

Make it your ambition to lead a quiet life,
to mind your own business and to work
with your hands, just as we told you.

Good News

1 Peter 1:3

Praise be to the God and Father
of our Lord Jesus Christ!
In his great mercy he has given us
new birth into a living hope
through the resurrection of Jesus
Christ from the dead.

John 3:16

For God so loved the world
that he gave his one and only Son,
that whoever believes in him
shall not perish but have eternal life.

John 3:36

Whoever believes in the Son
has eternal life.

Ephesians 2:13

Now in Christ Jesus you who once
were far away have been brought near
through the blood of Christ.

Romans 5:8

God demonstrates his own love for us
in this: While we were still sinners,
Christ died for us.

1 John 4:10

This is love: not that we loved God, but
that he loved us and sent his Son as an
atoning sacrifice for our sins.

Colossians 2:13-14

When you were dead in your sins and in
the uncircumcision of your sinful nature,
God made you alive with Christ.
He forgave us all our sins,
having canceled the written code,
with its regulations, that was against us
and that stood opposed to us;
he took it away, nailing it to the cross.

2 Corinthians 5:21

God made him who had no sin
to be sin for us, so that in him we might
become the righteousness of God.

GOODNESS

JAMES 3:13
Who is wise and understanding among you? Let him show it by his good life, by deeds done in the humility that comes from wisdom.

1 THESSALONIANS 5:21-22
Test everything. Hold on to the good. Avoid every kind of evil.

PSALM 37:3
Trust in the LORD and do good; dwell in the land and enjoy safe pasture.

3 JOHN 1:11
Anyone who does what is good is from God.

EPHESIANS 2:10
For we are God's workmanship, created in Christ Jesus to do good works, which God prepared in advance for us to do.

Matthew 5:16

Let your light shine before men, that
they may see your good deeds and
praise your Father in heaven.

Galatians 6:10

As we have opportunity, let us do good
to all people, especially to those who
belong to the family of believers.

Galatians 6:9

Let us not become weary in doing good,
for at the proper time we will reap a
harvest if we do not give up.

Ecclesiastes 3:12

I know that there is nothing better for
men than to be happy and do good while
they live.

Proverbs 12:2

A good man obtains favor from the LORD,
but the LORD condemns a crafty man.

Psalm 37:27

Turn from evil and do good;
then you will dwell in the land forever.

GOODNESS of GOD

PSALM 145:9

The LORD is good to all;
he has compassion on all he has made.

PSALM 25:8

Good and upright is the LORD;
therefore he instructs sinners in his ways.

NAHUM 1:7

The LORD is good,
a refuge in times of trouble.
He cares for those who trust in him.

PSALM 31:19

How great is your goodness,
which you have stored up
for those who fear you,
which you bestow in the sight of men
on those who take refuge in you.

LAMENTATIONS 3:25

The LORD is good to those whose hope
is in him, to the one who seeks him.

PSALM 27:13

I am still confident of this:
I will see the goodness of the LORD
in the land of the living.

2 PETER 1:3

His divine power
has given us everything we need
for life and godliness through
our knowledge of him who called us
by his own glory and goodness.

PSALM 16:2

I said to the LORD, "You are my Lord;
apart from you I have no good thing."

ROMANS 8:28

We know that in all things
God works for the good of those
who love him, who have been called
according to his purpose.

GRACE

ROMANS 5:17

For if, by the trespass of the one man,
death reigned through that one man,
how much more will those who receive
God's abundant provision of grace and
of the gift of righteousness reign in life
through the one man, Jesus Christ.

LAMENTATIONS 3:22

Because of the LORD's great love
we are not consumed,
for his compassions never fail.

EPHESIANS 2:6-7

God raised us up with Christ and seated
us with him in the heavenly realms in
Christ Jesus, in order that in the coming
ages he might show the incomparable
riches of his grace, expressed in
his kindness to us in Christ Jesus.

ROMANS 5:1-2

Since we have been justified through faith,
we have peace with God through our Lord
Jesus Christ, through whom
we have gained access by faith into this
grace in which we now stand. And we
rejoice in the hope of the glory of God.

PSALM 116:5

The LORD is gracious and righteous;
our God is full of compassion.

2 CORINTHIANS 8:9

For you know the grace of our Lord Jesus
Christ, that though he was rich, yet for
your sakes he became poor, so that you
through his poverty might become rich.

JOHN 1:16

From the fullness of his grace we have
all received one blessing after another.

2 CORINTHIANS 9:8

God is able to make all grace abound to
you, so that in all things at all times,
having all that you need, you will
abound in every good work.

2 CORINTHIANS 12:9

He said to me, "My grace is sufficient
for you, for my power is made perfect
in weakness." Therefore I will boast
all the more gladly about my weaknesses,
so that Christ's power may rest on me.

PETER 5:10

The God of all grace, who called you to
his eternal glory in Christ,
after you have suffered a little while,
will himself restore you and make you
strong, firm and steadfast.

2 PETER 1:2

Grace and peace be yours
in abundance through the knowledge
of God and of Jesus our Lord.

EPHESIANS 2:4–5

But because of his great love for us,
God, who is rich in mercy,
made us alive with Christ even when
we were dead in transgressions—
it is by grace you have been saved.

2 Timothy 1:8-10

So do not be ashamed to testify about
our Lord, or ashamed of me his prisoner.
But join with me in suffering for the
gospel, by the power of God, who has
saved us and called us to a holy life—
not because of anything we have done but
because of his own purpose and grace.
This grace was given us in Christ Jesus
before the beginning of time, but it has
now been revealed through the appearing
of our Savior, Christ Jesus, who has
destroyed death and has brought life and
immortality to light through the gospel.

Titus 3:5-7

He saved us, not because
of righteous things we had done,
but because of his mercy.
He saved us through the washing of
rebirth and renewal by the Holy Spirit,
whom he poured out on us generously
through Jesus Christ our Savior,
so that, having been justified by his grace,
we might become heirs
having the hope of eternal life.

GROWTH

PHILIPPIANS 1:9

This is my prayer: that your love
may abound more and more
in knowledge and depth of insight.

COLOSSIANS 1:10

We pray ... in order that you may live a life
worthy of the Lord and may please him
in every way: bearing fruit in every good
work, growing in the knowledge of God.

1 THESSALONIANS 4:1

Finally, brothers, we instructed you how
to live in order to please God,
as in fact you are living.
Now we ask you and urge you in
the Lord Jesus to do this more and more.

2 PETER 1:5-6

Make every effort to add to your faith
goodness; and to goodness, knowledge;
and to knowledge, self-control;
and to self-control, perseverance;
and to perseverance, godliness.

2 PETER 3:18

Grow in the grace and knowledge of
our Lord and Savior Jesus Christ.
To him be glory both now and forever!
Amen.

1 TIMOTHY 4:15

Be diligent in these matters;
give yourself wholly to them,
so that everyone may see your progress.

2 THESSALONIANS 1:3

We ought always to thank God for you,
brothers, and rightly so, because
your faith is growing more and more,
and the love every one of you
has for each other is increasing.

GUIDANCE

EXODUS 15:13

In your unfailing love you will lead
the people you have redeemed.
In your strength you will guide them
to your holy dwelling.

PSALM 48:14

For this God is our God for ever and ever;
he will be our guide even to the end.

PSALM 23:2-3

He makes me lie down in green pastures,
he leads me beside quiet waters,
he restores my soul.
He guides me in paths of righteousness
for his name's sake.

PROVERBS 4:11

I guide you in the way of wisdom
and lead you along straight paths.

ISAIAH 58:11

The LORD will guide you always;
he will satisfy your needs
in a sun-scorched land
and will strengthen your frame.
You will be like a well-watered garden,
like a spring whose waters never fail.

PSALM 139:9-10

If I rise on the wings of the dawn,
if I settle on the far side of the sea,
even there your hand will guide me,
your right hand will hold me fast.

PSALM 37:23-24

If the LORD delights in a man's way,
he makes his steps firm;
though he stumble, he will not fall,
for the LORD upholds him with his hand.

PROVERBS 3:5-6

Trust in the LORD with all your heart
and lean not on your own understanding;
in all your ways acknowledge him,
and he will make your paths straight.

ISAIAH 42:16

I will lead the blind
by ways they have not known,
along unfamiliar paths I will guide them;
I will turn the darkness into light before
them and make the rough places smooth.
These are the things I will do;
I will not forsake them.

JOHN 16:13

When he, the Spirit of truth, comes,
he will guide you into all truth.
He will not speak on his own;
he will speak only what he hears, and
he will tell you what is yet to come.

PSALM 107:30-32

They were glad when it grew calm,
and he guided them
to their desired haven.
Let them give thanks to the LORD
for his unfailing love
and his wonderful deeds for men.
Let them exalt him in the assembly of
the people and praise him
in the council of the elders.

JEREMIAH 29:11

"For I know the plans I have for you,"
declares the LORD, "plans to prosper you
and not to harm you, plans to give you
hope and a future."

PROVERBS 6:20-23

My son, keep your father's commands and
do not forsake your mother's teaching.
Bind them upon your heart forever;
fasten them around your neck.
When you walk, they will guide you;
when you sleep, they will watch over you;
when you awake, they will speak to you.
For these commands are a lamp,
this teaching is a light,
and the corrections of discipline
are the way to life,

JOHN 14:26

The Counselor, the Holy Spirit,
whom the Father will send in my name,
will teach you all things and will remind
you of everything I have said to you.

HEALING

JEREMIAH 33:6

I will heal my people and will let them
enjoy abundant peace and security.

HOSEA 14:4

I will heal their waywardness
and love them freely,
for my anger has turned away from them.

1 PETER 2:24

He himself bore our sins in his body
on the tree, so that we might die to sins
and live for righteousness;
by his wounds you have been healed.

PSALM 103:2-3

Praise the LORD, O my soul,
and forget not all his benefits—
who forgives all your sins
and heals all your diseases.

JEREMIAH 30:17

I will restore you to health
and heal your wounds,'
declares the LORD,
'because you are called an outcast,
Zion for whom no one cares.'

JEREMIAH 17:14

Heal me, O LORD, and I will be healed;
save me and I will be saved,
for you are the one I praise.

JAMES 5:15–16

The prayer offered in faith
will make the sick person well;
the Lord will raise him up.
If he has sinned, he will be forgiven.
Confess your sins to each other
and pray for each other
so that you may be healed.
The prayer of a righteous man
is powerful and effective.

PSALM 30:2

O LORD my God,
I called to you for help and you healed me.

HEAVEN

REVELATION 22:14
Blessed are those who wash their robes,
that they may have the right
to the tree of life and
may go through the gates into the city.

JOHN 14:2
In my Father's house are many rooms;
if it were not so, I would have told you.
I am going there
to prepare a place for you.

2 CORINTHIANS 5:1
Now we know that if the earthly tent
we live in is destroyed,
we have a building from God,
an eternal house in heaven,
not built by human hands.

LUKE 10:20
Rejoice that your names
are written in heaven.

Revelation 21:27

Nothing impure will ever enter it,
nor will anyone who does what is
shameful or deceitful,
but only those whose names are
written in the Lamb's book of life.

Revelation 21:4

He will wipe every tear from their eyes.
There will be no more death or mourning
or crying or pain, for the old order of
things has passed away.

Revelation 7:16-17

Never again will they hunger;
never again will they thirst.
The sun will not beat upon them,
nor any scorching heat.
For the Lamb at the center of the
throne will be their shepherd;
he will lead them
to springs of living water.
And God will wipe away every tear
from their eyes.

DANIEL 7:10

A river of fire was flowing,
coming out from before him.
Thousands upon thousands attended him;
ten thousand times
ten thousand stood before him.
The court was seated,
and the books were opened.

REVELATION 7:9

I looked and there before me was a
great multitude that no one could count,
from every nation, tribe, people
and language, standing before the throne
and in front of the Lamb.
They were wearing white robes and were
holding palm branches in their hands.

REVELATION 19:6

I heard what sounded like a great
multitude, like the roar of rushing waters
and like loud peals of thunder, shouting:
"Hallelujah!
For our Lord God Almighty reigns."

PHILIPPIANS 3:20

But our citizenship is in heaven.
And we eagerly await a Savior from
there, the Lord Jesus Christ,

1 THESSALONIANS 4:15-18

According to the Lord's own word,
we tell you that we who are still alive,
who are left till the coming of the Lord,
will certainly not precede
those who have fallen asleep.
For the Lord himself will come down
from heaven, with a loud command,
with the voice of the archangel
and with the trumpet call of God,
and the dead in Christ will rise first.
After that, we who are still alive
and are left will be caught up
together with them in the clouds
to meet the Lord in the air.
And so we will be with the Lord forever.
Therefore encourage each other
with these words.

HELP

HEBREWS 2:18

Because he himself suffered when he was tempted, he is able to help those who are being tempted.

PSALM 72:12

For he will deliver the needy who cry out, the afflicted who have no one to help.

PSALM 10:14

You, O God, do see trouble and grief; you consider it to take it in hand. The victim commits himself to you; you are the helper of the fatherless.

ISAIAH 59:1

Surely the arm of the LORD is not too short to save, nor his ear too dull to hear.

PSALM 46:1

God is our refuge and strength,
an ever-present help in trouble.

PSALM 28:7

The LORD is my strength and my shield;
my heart trusts in him, and I am helped.
My heart leaps for joy
and I will give thanks to him in song.

PSALM 68:19

Praise be to the Lord, to God our Savior,
who daily bears our burdens.

ISAIAH 50:9

It is the Sovereign LORD who helps me.
Who is he that will condemn me?
They will all wear out like a garment;
the moths will eat them up.

HEBREWS 13:6

So we say with confidence,
"The Lord is my helper;
I will not be afraid.
What can man do to me?"

HOLINESS

1 THESSALONIANS 5:23

May God himself, the God of peace,
sanctify you through and through. May
your whole spirit, soul and body be
kept blameless at the coming of our
Lord Jesus Christ.

1 PETER 1:15-16

Just as he who called you is holy, so be
holy in all you do; for it is written: "Be
holy, because I am holy."

1 THESSALONIANS 4:7

God did not call us to be impure, but to
live a holy life.

PSALM 84:11

For the LORD God is a sun and shield;
the LORD bestows favor and honor; no
good thing does he withhold from
those whose walk is blameless.

2 CORINTHIANS 7:1

Since we have these promises,
dear friends, let us purify ourselves
from everything that contaminates
body and spirit, perfecting holiness
out of reverence for God.

ROMANS 6:22

Now that you have been set free from
sin and have become slaves to God, the
benefit you reap leads to holiness, and
the result is eternal life.

EPHESIANS 1:4-6

He chose us in him before the creation of
the world to be holy and blameless in his
sight. In love he predestined us to be
adopted as his sons through Jesus Christ,
in accordance with his pleasure and
will—to the praise of his glorious grace,
which he has freely given us in the One
he loves.

HONESTY

PSALM 51:6

Surely you desire truth in the inner parts;
you teach me wisdom in the inmost place.

1 CORINTHIANS 13:6

Love ... rejoices with the truth.

EPHESIANS 6:14

Stand firm then,
with the belt of truth buckled around
your waist, with the breastplate of
righteousness in place.

TITUS 2:7-8

In everything set them an example
by doing what is good.
In your teaching show integrity, serious-
ness and soundness of speech that cannot
be condemned, so that those who oppose
you may be ashamed because
they have nothing bad to say about us.

PROVERBS 10:9

The man of integrity
walks securely, but he who takes
crooked paths will be found out.

PROVERBS 13:5

The righteous hate what is false.

PSALM 15:2, 5

He whose walk is blameless
and who does what is righteous,
who speaks the truth from his heart....
He who does these things
will never be shaken.

ISAIAH 33:15–16

He who walks righteously
and speaks what is right ... this is the man
who will dwell on the heights, whose
refuge will be the mountain fortress.
His bread will be supplied,
and water will not fail him.

PROVERBS 24:26

An honest answer
is like a kiss on the lips.

HOPE

1 TIMOTHY 4:9-10

This is a trustworthy saying that
deserves full acceptance
(and for this we labor and strive),
that we have put our hope in the living
God, who is the Savior of all men,
and especially of those who believe.

1 PETER 1:3

Praise be to the God and Father
of our Lord Jesus Christ!
In his great mercy he has given us
new birth into a living hope
through the resurrection of
Jesus Christ from the dead.

1 PETER 1:21

Through him you believe in God,
who raised him from the dead
and glorified him,
and so your faith and hope are in God.

ACTS 2:26-27

My heart is glad
and my tongue rejoices; my body also
will live in hope, because you will not
abandon me to the grave, nor will you
let your Holy One see decay.

LAMENTATIONS 3:21-22

This I call to mind and therefore
I have hope: Because of the LORD's
great love we are not consumed,
for his compassions never fail.

PSALM 147:11

The LORD delights in those who fear him,
who put their hope in his unfailing love.

LAMENTATIONS 3:25-26

The LORD is good to those whose hope
is in him, to the one who seeks him;
it is good to wait quietly
for the salvation of the LORD.

ROMANS 5:5

Hope does not disappoint us, because God
has poured out his love into our hearts by
the Holy Spirit, whom he has given us.

ISAIAH 40:31

Those who hope in the LORD
will renew their strength.
They will soar on wings like eagles;
they will run and not grow weary,
they will walk and not be faint.

PROVERBS 24:14

Know also that wisdom
is sweet to your soul;
if you find it,
there is a future hope for you,
and your hope will not be cut off.

PSALM 42:5-11

Why are you downcast, O my soul?
Why so disturbed within me?
Put your hope in God,
for I will yet praise him,
my Savior and my God.
My soul is downcast within me;
therefore I will remember you from the
land of the Jordan, the heights of
Hermon—from Mount Mizar.

Deep calls to deep
in the roar of your waterfalls;
all your waves and breakers
have swept over me.
By day the LORD directs his love,
at night his song is with me—
a prayer to the God of my life.
I say to God my Rock,
"Why have you forgotten me?
Why must I go about mourning,
oppressed by the enemy?"
My bones suffer mortal agony
as my foes taunt me,
saying to me all day long,
"Where is your God?"
Why are you downcast, O my soul?
Why so disturbed within me?
Put your hope in God,
for I will yet praise him,
my Savior and my God.

JEREMIAH 29:11

For I know the plans I have for you,"
declares the LORD,
"plans to prosper you
and not to harm you,
plans to give you hope and a future.

HOSPITALITY

TITUS 1:8

He must be hospitable, one who loves what is good, who is self-controlled, upright, holy and disciplined.

DEUTERONOMY 15:11

There will always be poor people in the land. Therefore I command you to be openhanded toward your brothers and toward the poor and needy in your land.

HEBREWS 13:2-3

Do not forget to entertain strangers, for by so doing some people have entertained angels without knowing it. Remember those in prison as if you were their fellow prisoners, and those who are mistreated as if you yourselves were suffering.

MATTHEW 10:42

If anyone gives even a cup of cold water to one of these little ones because he is my disciple, I tell you the truth, he will certainly not lose his reward.

MATTHEW 25:34-36

The king will say to those on his right, "Come, you who are blessed by my Father; take your inheritance, the kingdom prepared for you since the creation of the world. For I was hungry and you gave me something to eat, I was thirsty and you gave me something to drink, I was a stranger and you invited me in, I needed clothes and you clothed me, I was sick and you looked after me, I was in prison and you came to visit me."

1 PETER 4:9

Offer hospitality to one another without grumbling.

ROMANS 12:13

Share with God's people who are in need. Practice hospitality.

HUMILITY

PROVERBS 22:4
Humility and the fear of the LORD
bring wealth and honor and life.

JAMES 4:10
Humble yourselves before the Lord,
and he will lift you up.

PSALM 149:4
For the LORD takes delight in his people;
he crowns the humble with salvation.

PROVERBS 15:33
The fear of the LORD
teaches a man wisdom,
and humility comes before honor.

PSALM 147:6
The LORD sustains the humble
but casts the wicked to the ground.

Psalm 25:9

He guides the humble in what is right
and teaches them his way.

James 3:13

Who is wise and understanding
among you? Let him show it
by his good life, by deeds done
in the humility that comes from wisdom.

Matthew 18:4

Whoever humbles himself like this child
is the greatest in the kingdom of heaven.

Philippians 2:3

Do nothing out of selfish ambition
or vain conceit, but in humility consider
others better than yourselves.

Titus 3:1-2

Remind the people to be subject to rulers
and authorities, to be obedient,
to be ready to do whatever is good,
to slander no one, to be peaceable
and considerate, and to show
true humility toward all men.

HUSBANDS

EPHESIANS 5:25-28

Husbands, love your wives,
just as Christ loved the church and
gave himself up for her to make her holy,
cleansing her by the washing with
water through the word, and to present
her to himself as a radiant church,
without stain or wrinkle or
any other blemish, but holy and blameless.
In this same way, husbands ought to
love their wives as their own bodies.
He who loves his wife loves himself.

1 PETER 3:7

Husbands, in the same way be considerate
as you live with your wives, and treat
them with respect as the weaker partner
and as heirs with you of the gracious gift
of life, so that nothing
will hinder your prayers.

1 Corinthians 7:4

The wife's body does not belong to her
alone but also to her husband.
In the same way,
the husband's body does not belong to him
alone but also to his wife.

Colossians 3:19

Husbands, love your wives
and do not be harsh with them.

Proverbs 5:18-19

May your fountain be blessed,
and may you rejoice
in the wife of your youth.
A loving doe, a graceful deer—
may her breasts satisfy you always,
may you ever be captivated by her love.

Ecclesiastes 9:9

Enjoy life with your wife,
whom you love, all the days of
this meaningless life that
God has given you under the sun—
all your meaningless days.
For this is your lot in life and in your
toilsome labor under the sun.

IDENTITY

ISAIAH 43:1

Now, this is what the LORD says—
he who created you, O Jacob, he who
formed you, O Israel: "Fear not, for I
have redeemed you; I have summoned
you by name; you are mine."

PSALM 100:3

Know that the LORD is God.
It is he who made us, and we are his;
we are his people, the sheep of his pasture.

1 SAMUEL 12:22

For the sake of his great name the
LORD will not reject his people,
because the LORD was pleased
to make you his own.

COLOSSIANS 3:12

As God's chosen people, holy and dearly
loved, clothe yourselves with compassion,
kindness, humility, gentleness and patience.

1 Peter 2:9

You are a chosen people, a royal
priesthood, a holy nation, a people
belonging to God, that you may declare
the praises of him who called you
out of darkness into his wonderful light.

Psalm 95:6-7

Come, let us bow down in worship,
let us kneel before the LORD our Maker;
for he is our God
and we are the people of his pasture,
the flock under his care.

Ephesians 1:13

You also were included in Christ when
you heard the word of truth,
the gospel of your salvation.
Having believed, you were marked in him
with a seal, the promised Holy Spirit.

Ephesians 2:10

For we are God's workmanship, created
in Christ Jesus to do good works,
which God prepared in advance for us
to do.

INTEGRITY

1 CHRONICLES 29:17

I know, my God, that you test the heart
and are pleased with integrity.

PSALM 84:11

For the LORD God is a sun and shield;
the LORD bestows favor and honor;
no good thing does he withhold
from those whose walk is blameless.

PROVERBS 2:7-8

He holds victory in store for the upright,
he is a shield to those
whose walk is blameless,
for he guards the course of the just
and protects the way of his faithful ones.

PROVERBS 10:9

The man of integrity walks securely,
but he who takes crooked paths
will be found out.

PROVERBS 11:3

The integrity of the upright guides them,
but the unfaithful are
destroyed by their duplicity.

LUKE 16:10

Whoever can be trusted with very little
can also be trusted with much,
and whoever is dishonest with very little
will also be dishonest with much.

ISAIAH 57:2

Those who walk uprightly
enter into peace;
they find rest as they lie in death.

PROVERBS 16:7

When a man's ways
are pleasing to the LORD, he makes
even his enemies live at peace with
him.

JAMES 2:18

Someone will say,
"You have faith; I have deeds."
Show me your faith without deeds,
and I will show you my faith by what I do.

JOY

PSALM 19:8

The precepts of the LORD are right,
giving joy to the heart.
The commands of the LORD are radiant,
giving light to the eyes.

PSALM 92:4

For you make me glad
by your deeds, O LORD;
I sing for joy at the works of your hands.

PSALM 30:11–12

You turned my wailing into dancing;
you removed my sackcloth
and clothed me with joy,
that my heart may sing to you
and not be silent.
O LORD my God,
I will give you thanks forever.

HEBREWS 1:9

You have loved righteousness
and hated wickedness
therefore God, your God,
has set you above your companions
by anointing you
with the oil of joy.

ISAIAH 61:10

I delight greatly in the LORD;
my soul rejoices in my God.
For he has clothed me with garments of
salvation and arrayed me in a robe of
righteousness, as a bridegroom adorns
his head like a priest, and as a bride
adorns herself with her jewels.

PSALM 16:11

You have made known to me the path of
life; you will fill me with joy in your
presence, with eternal pleasures at your
right hand.

PSALM 21:6

Surely you have granted him eternal
blessings and made him glad with the
joy of your presence.

1 PETER 1:8-9

Though you have not seen him,
you love him; and even though you do not
see him now, you believe in him and are
filled with an inexpressible and glorious
joy, for you are receiving the goal of
your faith, the salvation of your souls.

JAMES 1:2-3

Consider it pure joy, my brothers,
whenever you face trials of many kinds,
because you know that the testing of
your faith develops perseverance.

JOHN 16:24

Until now you have not asked for
anything in my name. Ask and you will
receive, and your joy will be complete.

DEUTERONOMY 16:15

For seven days celebrate the
Feast to the LORD your God at
the place the LORD will choose.
For the LORD your God will bless you
in all your harvest and in all the work of
your hands, and your joy will be complete.

Tremble before him, all the earth!
The world is firmly established;
it cannot be moved.
Let the heavens rejoice,
let the earth be glad;
let them say among the nations,
"The LORD reigns!"
Let the sea resound, and all that is in it;
let the fields be jubilant,
and everything in them!
Then the trees of the forest will sing,
they will sing for joy before the LORD,
for he comes to judge the earth.

Acts 2:26-28

Therefore my heart is glad
and my tongue rejoices;
my body also will live in hope,
because you will not abandon me
to the grave, nor will you
let your Holy One see decay.
You have made known to me
the paths of life;
you will fill me with joy in your presence.

JUSTICE

MICAH 6:8
He has showed you,
O man, what is good.
And what does the LORD require of you?
To act justly and to love mercy
and to walk humbly
with your God.

ROMANS 2:13
For it is not those who hear the law
who are righteous in God's sight,
but it is those who obey the law who
will be declared righteous.

PSALM 37:28
For the LORD loves the just
and will not forsake his faithful ones.
They will be protected forever,
but the offspring of the wicked
will be cut off.

PROVERBS 2:7-8

He holds victory in store
for the upright,
he is a shield to those
whose walk is blameless,
for he guards the course of the just
and protects the way
of his faithful ones.

ISAIAH 1:17

Learn to do right!
Seek justice,
encourage the oppressed.
Defend the cause of the fatherless,
plead the case of the widow.

PROVERBS 31:8-9

Speak up for those
who cannot speak for themselves,
for the rights of all who are destitute.
Speak up and judge fairly;
defend the rights
of the poor and needy.

JUSTICE *of* GOD

PSALM 103:6
The LORD works righteousness and
justice for all the oppressed.

PSALM 111:7
The works of his hands are faithful
and just; all his precepts are
trustworthy.

EXODUS 34:6-7
The LORD, the LORD, the compassionate
and gracious God, slow to anger,
abounding in love and faithfulness,
maintaining love to thousands, and
forgiving wickedness, rebellion and sin.
Yet he does not leave the guilty
unpunished; he punishes the children and
their children for the sin of the fathers to
the third and fourth generation.

Isaiah 30:18

Yet the LORD longs to be gracious to you;
he rises to show you compassion.
For the LORD is a God of justice.
Blessed are all who wait for him!

Deuteronomy 32:4

He is the Rock, his works are perfect,
and all his ways are just.
A faithful God who does no wrong,
upright and just is he.

Psalm 67:4

May the nations be glad and sing for joy,
for you rule the peoples justly
and guide the nations of the earth.

2 Thessalonians 1:5

God's judgment is right, and as a result
you will be counted worthy of the kingdom
of God, for which you are suffering.

Psalm 11:7

For the LORD is righteous,
he loves justice;
upright men will see his face.

JUSTIFICATION

GALATIANS 3:24

The law was put in charge to lead us to
Christ that we might be justified by faith.

2 CORINTHIANS 5:21

God made him who had no sin
to be sin for us, so that in him we might
become the righteousness of God.

ROMANS 5:18-19

Just as the result of one trespass
was condemnation for all men, so also the
result of one act of righteousness was
justification that brings life for all men.
For just as through the disobedience of
the one man the many were made sinners,
so also through the obedience of the one
man the many will be made righteous.

1 CORINTHIANS 6:11

You were washed, you were sanctified, you were justified in the name of the Lord Jesus Christ and by the Spirit of our God.

GENESIS 15:6

Abram believed the LORD, and he credited it to him as righteousness.

ROMANS 5:1

Since we have been justified through faith, we have peace with God through our Lord Jesus Christ.

ROMANS 10:10

For it is with your heart that you believe and are justified, and it is with your mouth that you confess and are saved.

JAMES 2:24

You see that a person is justified by what he does and not by faith alone.

KINDNESS

PROVERBS 11:16
A kindhearted woman gains respect,
but ruthless men gain only wealth.

PROVERBS 11:17
A kind man benefits himself,
but a cruel man brings trouble on himself.

EPHESIANS 4:32
Be kind and compassionate to one
another, forgiving each other, just as
in Christ God forgave you.

COLOSSIANS 3:12
As God's chosen people, holy
and dearly loved, clothe yourselves
with compassion, kindness, humility,
gentleness and patience.

2 Peter 1:5-7

For this very reason, make every effort
to add to your faith goodness;
and to goodness, knowledge;
and to knowledge, self-control;
and to self-control, perseverance;
and to perseverance, godliness;
and to godliness, brotherly kindness;
and to brotherly kindness, love.

Matthew 7:12

So in everything, do to others
what you would have them do to you, for
this sums up the Law and the Prophets.

1 Thessalonians 5:15

Make sure that nobody
pays back wrong for wrong,
but always try to be kind to each other
and to everyone else.

1 Corinthians 13:4

Love is patient, love is kind.
It does not envy, it does not boast,
it is not proud.

KINDNESS *of* GOD

JEREMIAH 31:3

The LORD appeared to us in the past, saying:
"I have loved you with an everlasting love;
I have drawn you with loving-kindness."

ROMANS 11:22

Consider therefore the kindness
and sternness of God:
sternness to those who fell,
but kindness to you, provided
that you continue in his kindness.

ISAIAH 63:7

I will tell of the kindnesses of the LORD,
the deeds for which he is to be praised,
according to all the LORD has done
for us—yes, the many good things he has
done for the house of Israel, according to
his compassion and many kindnesses.

ROMANS 2:4

God's kindness leads you toward repentance.

Jeremiah 9:24

"Let him who boasts boast about this:
that he understands and knows me, that
I am the LORD, who exercises kindness,
justice and righteousness on earth,
for in these I delight," declares the LORD.

Job 10:12

You gave me life and showed me
kindness, and in your providence
watched over my spirit.

Titus 3:4-5

When the kindness and love of God our
Savior appeared, he saved us, not because
of righteous things we had done,
but because of his mercy.
He saved us through the washing of
rebirth and renewal by the Holy Spirit.

Ephesians 2:6-7

God raised us up with Christ and seated us
with him in the heavenly realms in
Christ Jesus, in order that in the coming
ages he might show the incomparable
riches of his grace, expressed in his
kindness to us in Christ Jesus.

KINGDOM *of* GOD

PSALM 103:19

The LORD has established his throne in
heaven, and his kingdom rules over all.

PSALM 45:6

Your throne, O God, will last for ever
and ever; a scepter of justice will be
the scepter of your kingdom.

DANIEL 7:27

Then the sovereignty, power and great-
ness of the kingdoms under the whole
heaven will be handed over to the saints,
the people of the Most High. His kingdom
will be an everlasting kingdom,
and all rulers will worship and obey him.

JOHN 18:36

Jesus said, "My kingdom is not
of this world ... But now my kingdom is
from another place."

LUKE 17:21

The kingdom of God is within you.

ROMANS 14:17

For the kingdom of God is not a matter of
eating and drinking, but of righteousness,
peace and joy in the Holy Spirit.

MATTHEW 4:17

Repent, for the kingdom of heaven is near.

LUKE 12:32

Do not be afraid, little flock,
for your Father has been pleased
to give you the kingdom.

COLOSSIANS 1:13–14

For he has rescued us from the dominion
of darkness and brought us into the
kingdom of the Son he loves, in whom we
have redemption, the forgiveness of sins.

HEBREWS 12:28

Since we are receiving a kingdom that
cannot be shaken, let us be thankful,
and so worship God acceptably
with reverence and awe.

LIFE

JOHN 6:35

Then Jesus declared, "I am the bread of life. He who comes to me will never go hungry, and he who believes in me will never be thirsty."

JOHN 11:25-26

Jesus said to her, "I am the resurrection and the life. He who believes in me will live, even though he dies; and whoever lives and believes in me will never die. Do you believe this?"

ROMANS 6:11

Count yourselves dead to sin but alive to God in Christ Jesus.

JOB 33:4

The Spirit of God has made me; the breath of the Almighty gives me life.

Romans 8:2

Through Christ Jesus the law of the
Spirit of life set me free from the law
of sin and death.

John 6:63

The Spirit gives life; the flesh counts
for nothing. The words I have spoken
to you are spirit and they are life.

Romans 8:11

If the Spirit of him who raised Jesus
from the dead is living in you, he who
raised Christ from the dead will also
give life to your mortal bodies through
his Spirit, who lives in you.

Acts 2:28

You have made known to me the paths of
life; you will fill me with joy in your
presence.

Proverbs 3:1-2

My son, do not forget my teaching,
but keep my commands in your heart,
for they will prolong your life many years
and bring you prosperity.

LOVE *for* GOD

MARK 12:29–31

"The most important one,"
answered Jesus, "is this: 'Hear, O Israel,
the Lord our God, the Lord is one.
Love the Lord your God with all your
heart and with all your soul an with
all your mind and with all your strength.'
The second is this: 'Love your neighbor
as yourself.' There is no commandment
greater than these."

MATTHEW 22:37

Jesus replied:
" 'Love the Lord your God with
all your heart and with all your soul
and with all your mind.' "

DEUTERONOMY 30:20

Love the LORD your God,
listen to his voice, and hold fast to him.
For the LORD is your life.

Psalm 31:23

Love the LORD, all his saints!
The LORD preserves the faithful,
but the proud he pays back in full.

1 John 5:3

This is love for God:
to obey his commands.
And his commands are not burdensome.

John 14:21

Whoever has my commands and obeys
them, he is the one who loves me. He who
loves me will be loved by my Father, and I
too will love him and show myself to him.

John 14:23

Jesus replied, "If anyone loves me, he
will obey my teaching. My Father will
love him, and we will come to him and
make our home with him."

Psalm 91:14

"Because he loves me,"
says the LORD, "I will rescue him;
I will protect him,
for he acknowledges my name."

LOVE *for* OTHERS

JAMES 2:8

If you really keep the royal law found
in Scripture, "Love your neighbor
as yourself," you are doing right.

1 JOHN 4:19

We love because he first loved us.

1 JOHN 4:7

Dear friends, let us love one another,
for love comes from God. Everyone who
loves has been born of God and knows God.

MATTHEW 5:44-45

I tell you: Love your enemies
and pray for those who persecute you,
that you may be sons
of your Father in heaven.

Proverbs 17:9

He who covers over an offense
promotes love, but whoever repeats
the matter separates close friends.

Hebrews 13:1

Keep on loving each other as brothers.

1 Thessalonians 4:9-10

Now about brotherly love we do not need to
write to you, for you yourselves
have been taught by God to love each other.
And in fact, you do love all the brothers
throughout Macedonia. Yet we urge you,
brothers, to do so more and more.

1 John 2:10

Whoever loves his brother lives
in the light, and there is nothing
in him to make him stumble.

1 John 4:18

There is no fear in love.
But perfect love drives out fear,
because fear has to do with punishment.
The one who fears
is not made perfect in love.

LOVE *of* GOD

PSALM 145:8
The LORD is gracious and compassionate,
slow to anger and rich in love.

PSALM 107:8-9
Let them give thanks to the LORD
for his unfailing love and his wonderful
deeds for men, for he satisfies the thirsty
and fills the hungry with good things.

JEREMIAH 31:3
The LORD appeared to us in the past, saying:
"I have loved you with an everlasting love;
I have drawn you with loving-kindness."

ISAIAH 54:10
"Though the mountains be shaken
and the hills be removed,
yet my unfailing love for you
will not be shaken nor my covenant
of peace be removed," says the LORD,
who has compassion on you.

PSALM 103:17

From everlasting to everlasting
the LORD's love is with those
who fear him, and his righteousness
with their children's children.

HOSEA 2:19-20

I will betroth you to me forever;
I will betroth you in righteousness
and justice, in love and compassion.
I will betroth you in faithfulness,
and you will acknowledge the LORD.

EPHESIANS 2:4-5

Because of his great love for us,
God, who is rich in mercy, made us
alive with Christ even when we
were dead in transgressions—
it is by grace you have been saved.

LAMENTATIONS 3:22-23

Because of the LORD's great love
we are not consumed,
for his compassions never fail.
They are new every morning;
great is your faithfulness.

MARRIAGE

GENESIS 2:18

The LORD God said,
"It is not good for the man to be alone.
I will make a helper suitable for him."

ECCLESIASTES 4:9-10

Two are better than one,
because they have a good return
for their work:
If one falls down,
his friend can help him up.
But pity the man who falls
and has no one to help him up!

GENESIS 2:24

For this reason a man will leave his
father and mother and be united to his
wife, and they will become one flesh.

MARK 10:8-9

"The two will become one flesh."
So they are no longer two, but one.
Therefore what God has joined together,
let man not separate.

1 CORINTHIANS 7:3

The husband should fulfill
his marital duty to his wife,
and likewise the wife to her husband.

HEBREWS 13:4

Marriage should be honored by all,
and the marriage bed kept pure,
for God will judge the adulterer and
all the sexually immoral.

PROVERBS 5:15

Drink water from your own cistern,
running water from your own well.

COLOSSIANS 3:18-19

Wives, submit to your husbands,
as is fitting in the Lord.
Husbands, love your wives
and do not be harsh with them.

MATURITY

1 PETER 2:2

Like newborn babies,
crave pure spiritual milk, so that by it
you may grow up in your salvation.

PROVERBS 9:9

Instruct a wise man and he will be
wiser still; teach a righteous man and
he will add to his learning.

PSALM 90:12

Teach us to number our days aright,
that we may gain a heart of wisdom.

ISAIAH 43:18-19

Forget the former things;
do not dwell on the past.
See, I am doing a new thing!
Now it springs up; do you not perceive
it? I am making a way in the desert
and streams in the wasteland.

PHILIPPIANS 2:13

It is God who works in you to will and
to act according to his good purpose.

PHILIPPIANS 1:6

He who began a good work
in you will carry it on to completion
until the day of Christ Jesus.

EPHESIANS 4:11–13

It was he who gave some
to be apostles, some to be prophets,
some to be evangelists, and some to be
pastors and teachers, to prepare God's
people for works of service,
so that the body of Christ may be built
up until we all reach unity in the faith
and in the knowledge of the Son of God
and become mature, attaining to the
whole measure of the fullness of Christ.

JAMES 1:4

Perseverance must finish its work
so that you may be mature and complete,
not lacking anything.

MEDITATION

JOSHUA 1:8
Do not let this Book of the Law depart
from your mouth; meditate on it day
and night, so that you may be careful to
do everything written in it. Then you
will be prosperous and successful.

PSALM 1:1-2
Blessed is the man
who does not walk in the counsel of the
wicked or stand in the way of sinners
or sit in the seat of mockers.
But his delight is in the law of the LORD,
and on his law he meditates day and night.

PSALM 119:97
Oh, how I love your law!
I meditate on it all day long.

PSALM 77:12
I will meditate on all your works
and consider all your mighty deeds.

Psalm 119:147-148

I rise before dawn and cry for help;
I have put my hope in your word.
My eyes stay open through
the watches of the night, that I may
meditate on your promises.

Psalm 48:9

Within your temple, O God,
we meditate on your unfailing love.

Psalm 104:33-34

I will sing to the LORD all my life;
I will sing praise to my God
as long as I live.
May my meditation be pleasing to him,
as I rejoice in the LORD.

Psalm 19:14

May the words of my mouth
and the meditation of my heart
be pleasing in your sight,
O LORD, my Rock and my Redeemer.

MEN

1 CORINTHIANS 11:3

Now I want you to realize
that the head of every man is Christ,
and the head of the woman is man,
and the head of Christ is God.

1 TIMOTHY 2:8

I want men everywhere to lift up holy
hands in prayer, without anger or disput-
ing.

PSALM 112:1

Blessed is the man who fears the LORD,
who finds great delight in his commands.

1 PETER 5:5

Young men, in the same way be submissive
to those who are older. All of you, clothe
yourselves with humility toward one
another, because, "God opposes the proud
but gives grace to the humble."

1 TIMOTHY 6:11

You, man of God,
...pursue righteousness, godliness,
faith, love, endurance and gentleness.

PROVERBS 14:15-16

A prudent man gives thought to his steps.
A wise man fears the LORD and shuns evil,
but a fool is hotheaded and reckless.

PROVERBS 11:17

A kind man benefits himself,
but a cruel man brings trouble on himself.

PSALM 119:9

How can a young man keep his way pure?
By living according to your word.

TITUS 2:6

Encourage the young men
to be self-controlled.

TITUS 2:2

Teach the older men to be temperate,
worthy of respect, self-controlled, and
sound in faith, in love and in endurance.

MERCY *of* GOD

JAMES 5:11

The Lord is full of compassion and
mercy.

PSALM 145:8

The LORD is gracious and compassionate,
slow to anger and rich in love.

ISAIAH 55:6-7

Seek the LORD while he may be found;
call on him while he is near.
Let the wicked forsake his way
and the evil man his thoughts.
Let him turn to the LORD,
and he will have mercy on him,
and to our God, for he will freely pardon.

LUKE 1:50

His mercy extends to those who fear him,
from generation to generation.

PSALM 6:9

The LORD has heard my cry for mercy;
the LORD accepts my prayer.

PSALM 5:7

I, by your great mercy, will come into
your house; in reverence
will I bow down toward your holy temple.

1 PETER 1:3

Praise be to the God and Father
of our Lord Jesus Christ!
In his great mercy he has given us
new birth into a living hope
through the resurrection
of Jesus Christ from the dead.

TITUS 3:5

He saved us, not because
of righteous things we had done,
but because of his mercy.
He saved us through the washing
of rebirth and renewal by the Holy Spirit.

NATURE

PSALM 65:13
The meadows are covered with flocks
and the valleys are mantled with grain;
they shout for joy and sing.

PSALM 102:25
In the beginning you laid the foundations
of the earth, and the heavens
are the work of your hands.

NEHEMIAH 9:6
You alone are the LORD.
You made the heavens, even the highest
heavens, and all their starry host,
the earth and all that is on it,
the seas and all that is in them.
You give life to everything
and the multitudes of heaven worship you.

ISAIAH 44:23

Sing for joy, O heavens,
for the LORD has done this;
shout aloud, O earth beneath.
Burst into song, you mountains,
you forests and all your trees,
for the LORD has redeemed Jacob,
he displays his glory in Israel.

PSALM 69:34

Let heaven and earth praise him,
the seas and all that move in them.

PSALM 19:1

The heavens declare the glory of God;
the skies proclaim the work of his hands.

JOB 26:7

He spreads out the northern skies
over empty space;
he suspends the earth over nothing.

NEW LIFE

2 CORINTHIANS 5:17

If anyone is in Christ, he is a new creation; the old has gone, the new has come!

EZEKIEL 11:19

I will give them an undivided heart
and put a new spirit in them;
I will remove from them their heart of
stone and give them a heart of flesh.

ROMANS 6:4

We were therefore buried with him
through baptism into death
in order that, just as Christ was raised
from the dead through the glory of
the Father, we too may live a new life.

EZEKIEL 36:26

I will give you a new heart and put a new
spirit in you; I will remove from you your
heart of stone and give you a heart of flesh.

John 11:25-26

Jesus said to her,
"I am the resurrection and the life.
He who believes in me will live,
even though he dies;
and whoever lives
and believes in me will never die.
Do you believe this?"

Ephesians 2:4-5

Because of his great love for us,
God, who is rich in mercy,
made us alive with Christ even when we
were dead in transgressions—
it is by grace you have been saved.

Ephesians 4:24

Put on the new self, created to be like God
in true righteousness and holiness.

Colossians 3:9-10

You have taken off your old self with its
practices and have put on the new self,
which is being renewed in knowledge in
the image of its Creator.

OBEDIENCE

ROMANS 2:13

For it is not those who hear the law
who are righteous in God's sight,
but it is those who obey the law who
will be declared righteous.

LUKE 11:28

He replied, "Blessed rather are those
who hear the word of God and obey it."

MATTHEW 5:19

Whoever practices and teaches these
commands will be called great in the
kingdom of heaven.

DEUTERONOMY 13:4

It is the LORD your God you must follow,
and him you must revere.
Keep his commands and obey him;
serve him and hold fast to him.

JOHN 15:10-11

If you obey my commands,
you will remain in my love, just as
I have obeyed my Father's commands
and remain in his love. I have told you
this so that my joy may be in you
and that your joy may be complete.

1 JOHN 2:5

If anyone obeys his word,
God's love is truly made complete in
him. This is how we know we are in him.

JOB 36:11

If they obey and serve him,
they will spend the rest of their days
in prosperity and their years
in contentment.

PARENTS

PROVERBS 20:7
The righteous man leads a blameless life;
blessed are his children after him.

PSALM 103:17
From everlasting to everlasting
the LORD's love is with those
who fear him, and his righteousness
with their children's children.

DEUTERONOMY 4:40
Keep his decrees and commands,
which I am giving you today,
so that it may go well with you and your
children after you and that you may live
long in the land the LORD your God
gives you for all time.

PROVERBS 22:6
Train a child in the way he should go,
and when he is old he will not turn from it.

PROVERBS 29:17

Discipline your son,
and he will give you peace;
he will bring delight to your soul.

PROVERBS 29:15

The rod of correction imparts wisdom,
but a child left to himself
disgraces his mother.

ISAIAH 54:13

All your sons
will be taught by the LORD,
and great will be your children's peace.

DEUTERONOMY 6:6-7

These commandments that I give you
today are to be upon your hearts.
Impress them on your children.
Talk about them when you sit at home
and when you walk along the road,
when you lie down and when you get up.

PROVERBS 17:6

Children's children are a crown to the
aged, and parents are the pride of their
children.

PATIENCE

ROMANS 12:12

Be joyful in hope, patient in affliction,
faithful in prayer.

PSALM 40:1

I waited patiently for the LORD;
he turned to me and heard my cry.

PSALM 37:7

Be still before the LORD and wait
patiently for him;
do not fret when men
succeed in their ways,
when they carry out their wicked
schemes.

COLOSSIANS 3:13

Bear with each other
and forgive whatever grievances
you may have against one another.
Forgive as the Lord forgave you.

PROVERBS 19:11

A man's wisdom gives him patience;
it is to his glory to overlook an offense.

EPHESIANS 4:2

Be completely humble and gentle;
be patient,
bearing with one another in love.

PROVERBS 12:16

A fool shows his annoyance at once,
but a prudent man overlooks an insult.

1 THESSALONIANS 5:14

We urge you, brothers,
warn those who are idle,
encourage the timid, help the weak,
be patient with everyone.

PROVERBS 14:29

A patient man has great understanding,
but a quick-tempered man
displays folly.

PEACE

ROMANS 5:1
Since we have been justified through
faith, we have peace with God through
our Lord Jesus Christ.

PSALM 85:8
I will listen to what God the LORD
will say; he promises peace
to his people, his saints.

PSALM 119:165
Great peace have they who love your law,
and nothing can make them stumble.

ISAIAH 26:3
You will keep in perfect peace him whose
mind is steadfast, because he trusts in you.

JAMES 3:18
Peacemakers who sow in peace
raise a harvest of righteousness.

PHILIPPIANS 4:6–7

In everything, by prayer and petition,
with thanksgiving, present your requests
to God. And the peace of God,
which transcends all understanding,
will guard your hearts and your minds
in Christ Jesus.

ROMANS 8:6

The mind controlled by the Spirit
is life and peace.

PROVERBS 16:7

When a man's ways are pleasing
to the LORD, he makes even his
enemies live at peace with him.

MATTHEW 5:9

Blessed are the peacemakers,
for they will be called sons of God.

2 CORINTHIANS 13:11

Finally, brothers, good-by. Aim for
perfection, listen to my appeal, be of one
mind, live in peace. And the God of love
and peace will be with you.

PERSEVERANCE

JAMES 1:12

Blessed is the man who perseveres under
trial, because when he has stood the test,
he will receive the crown of life that God
has promised to those who love him.

1 PETER 5:10

The God of all grace, who called you to
his eternal glory in Christ,
after you have suffered a little while,
will himself restore you and make you
strong, firm and steadfast.

2 CORINTHIANS 4:17

For our light and momentary troubles
are achieving for us an eternal glory
that far outweighs them all.

PSALM 119:50

My comfort in my suffering is this:
Your promise preserves my life.

ROMANS 2:7

To those who by persistence in doing good
seek glory, honor and immortality,
he will give eternal life.

PSALM 17:5

My steps have held to your paths;
my feet have not slipped.

JAMES 1:4–5

Perseverance must finish its work
so that you may be mature and complete,
not lacking anything.

GALATIANS 6:9

Let us not become weary in doing good,
for at the proper time we will reap a
harvest if we do not give up.

PSALM 126:5

Those who sow in tears
will reap with songs of joy.

PROVERBS 14:23

All hard work brings a profit,
but mere talk leads only to poverty.

PRAISE

1 CHRONICLES 16:25

For great is the LORD
and most worthy of praise;
he is to be feared above all gods.

PSALM 103:2-4

Praise the LORD, O my soul,
and forget not all his benefits—
who forgives all your sins
and heals all your diseases,
who redeems your life from the pit
and crowns you with love and compassion.

2 SAMUEL 22:47

The LORD lives! Praise be to my Rock!
Exalted be God, the Rock, my Savior!

PSALM 139:14

I praise you because I am fearfully
and wonderfully made; your works
are wonderful, I know that full well.

1 Peter 1:3

Praise be to the God and Father
of our Lord Jesus Christ!
In his great mercy he has given us
new birth into a living hope
through the resurrection
of Jesus Christ from the dead.

Psalm 28:6

Praise be to the LORD,
for he has heard my cry for mercy.

Psalm 52:9

I will praise you forever
for what you have done; in your name
I will hope, for your name is good.
I will praise you
in the presence of your saints.

Psalm 9:1–2

I will praise you, O LORD,
with all my heart;
I will tell of all your wonders.
I will be glad and rejoice in you;
I will sing praise to your name,
O Most High.

PRAYER

1 THESSALONIANS 5:17
Pray continually.

COLOSSIANS 4:2
Devote yourselves to prayer, being
watchful and thankful.

MATTHEW 26:41
Watch and pray so that
you will not fall into temptation.
The spirit is willing, but the body is weak.

EPHESIANS 6:18
Pray in the Spirit on all occasions
with all kinds of prayers and requests.
With this in mind, be alert and always
keep on praying for all the saints.

JEREMIAH 29:12
You will call upon me and come and
pray to me, and I will listen to you.

DEUTERONOMY 4:7

What other nation is so great
as to have their gods near them
the way the LORD our God is near us
whenever we pray to him?

2 CHRONICLES 7:14

If my people,
who are called by my name,
will humble themselves and pray
and seek my face and turn from their
wicked ways, then will I hear
from heaven and will forgive their sin
and will heal their land.

JAMES 5:15

The prayer offered in faith
will make the sick person well;
the Lord will raise him up.
If he has sinned, he will be forgiven.

MARK 11:25

When you stand praying,
if you hold anything against anyone,
forgive him, so that your Father in heaven
may forgive you your sins.

PRESENCE *of* GOD

PSALM 145:18

The LORD is near to all who call on
him, to all who call on him in truth.

ACTS 17:27

[People] reach out for [God] and find him,
though he is not far from each one of us.

PSALM 139:9-10

If I rise on the wings of the dawn,
if I settle on the far side of the sea,
even there your hand will guide me,
your right hand will hold me fast.

HEBREWS 13:5

Never will I leave you;
never will I forsake you.

EXODUS 33:14

The LORD replied, "My Presence will
go with you, and I will give you rest."

PSALM 23:4

Even though I walk
through the valley of the
shadow of death,
I will fear no evil,
for you are with me;
your rod and your staff,
they comfort me.

ISAIAH 43:2-3

When you pass through the waters,
I will be with you;
and when you pass through the rivers,
they will not sweep over you.
When you walk through the fire,
you will not be burned;
the flames will not set you ablaze.
For I am the LORD, your God,
the Holy One of Israel, your Savior.

DEUTERONOMY 31:6

Be strong and courageous.
Do not be afraid or terrified
because of them,
for the LORD your God goes with you;
he will never leave you nor forsake you.

PRIORITIES

MATTHEW 6:33
Seek first his kingdom
and his righteousness, and all these
things will be given to you as well.

ECCLESIASTES 12:13
Now all has been heard;
here is the conclusion of the matter:
Fear God and keep his commandments,
for this is the whole duty of man.

2 CORINTHIANS 5:9
We make it our goal to please him,
whether we are at home in the body
or away from it.

2 TIMOTHY 2:22
Flee the evil desires of youth, and pursue righteousness, faith, love and
peace, along with those who call on the
Lord out of a pure heart.

MATTHEW 6:24

No one can serve two masters.
Either he will hate the one and love
the other, or he will be devoted
to the one and despise the other.
You cannot serve both God and Money.

PROVERBS 21:21

He who pursues righteousness and love
finds life, prosperity and honor.

1 PETER 2:2

Like newborn babies,
crave pure spiritual milk, so that by it
you may grow up in your salvation.

PHILIPPIANS 3:13-14

Brothers, I do not consider myself yet to
have taken hold of it. But one thing I do:
Forgetting what is behind and straining
toward what is ahead, I press on toward
the goal to win the prize for which God
has called me heavenward in Christ Jesus.

1 KINGS 22:5

But Jehoshaphat also said to the king of
Israel, "First seek the counsel of the LORD."

PROTECTION

PSALM 55:22

Cast your cares on the LORD
and he will sustain you;
he will never let the righteous fall.

PSALM 37:28

For the LORD loves the just and will not
forsake his faithful ones.
They will be protected forever, but the
offspring of the wicked will be cut off.

PSALM 91:14-15

"Because he loves me," says the LORD,
"I will rescue him; I will protect him,
for he acknowledges my name.
He will call upon me, and I will answer him;
I will be with him in trouble,
I will deliver him and honor him."

DEUTERONOMY 33:27

The eternal God is your refuge,
and underneath are the everlasting arms.
He will drive out your enemy before you,
saying, "Destroy him!"

2 SAMUEL 22:31

The LORD is a shield for all
who take refuge in him.

PROVERBS 2:7-8

He holds victory in store
for the upright, he is a shield to those
whose walk is blameless, for he guards
the course of the just and
protects the way of his faithful ones.

PSALM 32:7

You are my hiding place;
you will protect me from trouble and
surround me with songs of deliverance.

2 THESSALONIANS 3:3

The Lord is faithful,
and he will strengthen and protect you
from the evil one.

PROVISION of GOD

PHILIPPIANS 4:19
My God will meet all your needs
according to his glorious riches
in Christ Jesus.

PSALM 23:1
The LORD is my shepherd,
I shall not be in want.

JOEL 2:23
Be glad, O people of Zion,
rejoice in the LORD your God,
for he has given you
the autumn rains in righteousness.
He sends you abundant showers, both
autumn and spring rains, as before.

PSALM 111:5
He provides food for those who fear him;
he remembers his covenant forever.

Psalm 132:15

I will bless her with abundant provisions;
her poor will I satisfy with food.

Jeremiah 31:14

"I will satisfy the priests with abundance,
and my people will be filled
with my bounty," declares the LORD.

Acts 14:17

He has shown kindness by giving you rain
from heaven and crops in their seasons;
he provides you with plenty of food and
fills your hearts with joy.

1 Timothy 6:17

Command those who are rich
in this present world...
to put their hope in God,
who richly provides us with everything
for our enjoyment.

2 Corinthians 9:8

God is able to make all grace abound
to you, so that in all things at all times,
having all that you need,
you will abound in every good work.

2 CORINTHIANS 12:9

He said to me,
"My grace is sufficient for you,
for my power
is made perfect in weakness."
Therefore I will boast all the more
gladly about my weaknesses,
so that Christ's power may rest on me.

MATTHEW 6:30-32

If that is how God clothes
the grass of the field,
which is here today and tomorrow is
thrown into the fire,
will he not much more clothe you,
O you of little faith?
So do not worry, saying,
'What shall we eat?' or
What shall we drink?' or
What shall we wear?'
For the pagans run after all these things,
and your heavenly Father
knows that you need them.

MATTHEW 7:9–11

Which of you, if his son asks for bread,
will give him a stone?
Or if he asks for a fish,
will give him a snake?
If you, then, though you are evil,
know how to give good gifts
to your children, how much more
will your Father in heaven
give good gifts to those who ask him!

ISAIAH 58:11

The LORD will guide you always;
he will satisfy your needs
in a sun-scorched land
and will strengthen your frame.
You will be like a well-watered garden,
like a spring whose waters never fail.

PURIFICATION

Psalm 51:7
Cleanse me with hyssop, and I will be clean;
wash me, and I will be whiter than snow.

Psalm 51:10
Create in me a pure heart, O God,
and renew a steadfast spirit within me.

Isaiah 1:18
"Come now, let us reason together,"
says the LORD. "Though your sins are like
scarlet, they shall be as white as snow;
though they are red as crimson,
they shall be like wool."

1 John 1:9
If we confess our sins, he is faithful
and just and will forgive us our sins
and purify us from all unrighteousness.

EZEKIEL 36:25-27

I will sprinkle clean water on you,
and you will be clean;
I will cleanse you from all your impurities
and from all your idols.
I will give you a new heart
and put a new spirit in you;
I will remove from you your heart of stone
and give you a heart of flesh.
And I will put my Spirit in you
and move you to follow my decrees
and be careful to keep my laws.

1 JOHN 1:7

If we walk in the light, as he is
in the light, we have fellowship
with one another, and the blood of Jesus,
his Son, purifies us from all sin.

1 CORINTHIANS 6:11

You were washed, you were sanctified, you
were justified in the name of the Lord
Jesus Christ and by the Spirit of our God.

PURITY

PSALM 15:1-2

LORD, who may dwell in your sanctuary?
Who may live on your holy hill?
He whose walk is blameless
and who does what is righteous,
who speaks the truth from his heart.

PSALM 24:3-4

Who may ascend the hill of the LORD?
Who may stand in his holy place?
He who has clean hands
and a pure heart.

MATTHEW 5:8

Blessed are the pure in heart,
for they will see God.

PSALM 73:1

Surely God is good to Israel,
to those who are pure in heart.

PROVERBS 22:11

He who loves a pure heart
and whose speech is gracious
will have the king for his friend.

PSALM 18:24

The LORD has rewarded me
according to my righteousness,
according to the cleanness
of my hands in his sight.

1 TIMOTHY 4:12

Set an example for the believers
in speech, in life, in love,
in faith and in purity.

1 TIMOTHY 5:22

Keep yourself pure.

PSALM 119:9, 11

How can a young man keep his way pure?
By living according to your word...
I have hidden your word in my heart
that I might not sin against you.

PURSUIT

HEBREWS 12:2-3

Let us fix our eyes on Jesus,
the author and perfecter of our faith,
who for the joy set before him
endured the cross, scorning its shame,
and sat down at the right hand
of the throne of God.
Consider him who endured such
opposition from sinful men,
so that you will not grow weary
and lose heart.

1 TIMOTHY 4:9-10

This is a trustworthy saying
that deserves full acceptance
(and for this we labor and strive),
that we have put our hope
in the living God,
who is the Savior of all men,
and especially of those who believe.

Luke 12:31

Seek his kingdom, and these things
will be given to you as well.

Amos 5:14

Seek good, not evil, that you may live.
Then the LORD God Almighty will be
with you, just as you say he is.

Jeremiah 29:13

You will seek me and find me when you
seek me with all your heart.

Lamentations 3:25

The LORD is good to those
whose hope is in him,
to the one who seeks him.

Galatians 6:8

The one who sows to please the Spirit,
from the Spirit will reap eternal life.

Psalm 14:2

The LORD looks down from heaven
on the sons of men
to see if there are any who understand,
any who seek God.

QUIETNESS

ISAIAH 30:15

This is what the Sovereign LORD, the
Holy One of Israel, says:
"In repentance and rest is your salvation,
in quietness and trust is your strength."

PSALM 131:2

I have stilled and quieted my soul;
like a weaned child with its mother,
like a weaned child is my soul within me.

LAMENTATIONS 3:24-26

I say to myself,
"The LORD is my portion;
therefore I will wait for him.
The LORD is good to those whose hope
is in him, to the one who seeks him;
it is good to wait quietly
for the salvation of the LORD."

PSALM 37:7

Be still before the LORD and wait
patiently for him.

EXODUS 14:14

The LORD will fight for you;
you need only to be still.

PSALM 46:10

Be still, and know that I am God;
I will be exalted among the nations,
I will be exalted in the earth.

JOB 6:24

Teach me, and I will be quiet;
show me where I have been wrong.

ISAIAH 32:17

The fruit of righteousness will be peace;
the effect of righteousness
will be quietness and confidence forever.

1 PETER 3:4

It should be that of your inner self,
the unfading beauty of a gentle and
quiet spirit, which is of great worth
in God's sight.

REBIRTH

1 PETER 1:3

Praise be to the God and Father
of our Lord Jesus Christ!
In his great mercy he has given us new
birth into a living hope
through the resurrection
of Jesus Christ from the dead.

TITUS 3:5

He saved us, not because of righteous
things we had done,
but because of his mercy.
He saved us through the washing of
rebirth and renewal by the Holy Spirit.

COLOSSIANS 2:13

When you were dead in your sins and in
the uncircumcision of your sinful nature,
God made you alive with Christ.
He forgave us all our sins.

John 1:12-13

Yet to all who received him, to those
who believed in his name, he gave
the right to become children of God—
children born not of natural descent,
nor of human decision
or a husband's will, but born of God.

John 3:6

Flesh gives birth to flesh, but the
Spirit gives birth to spirit.

1 John 4:7

Dear friends, let us love one another,
for love comes from God.
Everyone who loves
has been born of God and knows God.

2 Corinthians 5:17

If anyone is in Christ, he is a new creation; the old has gone, the new has come!

Ezekiel 11:19

I will give them an undivided heart and
put a new spirit in them;
I will remove from them their heart
of stone and give them a heart of flesh.

REDEMPTION

GALATIANS 3:13

Christ redeemed us from the curse of the law by becoming a curse for us, for it is written: "Cursed is everyone who is hung on a tree."

1 PETER 1:18-19

For you know that it was not with perishable things such as silver or gold that you were redeemed from the empty way of life handed down to you from your forefathers, but with the precious blood of Christ, a lamb without blemish or defect.

HEBREWS 9:12

He did not enter by means of the blood of goats and calves; but he entered the Most Holy Place once for all by his own blood, having obtained eternal redemption.

EPHESIANS 1:7

In him we have redemption through his blood, the forgiveness of sins, in accordance with the riches of God's grace.

1 CORINTHIANS 1:30

It is because of him that you are in Christ Jesus, who has become for us wisdom from God—that is, our righteousness, holiness and redemption.

COLOSSIANS 1:13–14

For he has rescued us from the dominion of darkness and brought us into the kingdom of the Son he loves, in whom we have redemption, the forgiveness of sins.

LAMENTATIONS 3:57–58

You came near when I called you, and you said, "Do not fear." O Lord, you took up my case; you redeemed my life.

ISAIAH 44:22

I have swept away your offenses like a cloud, your sins like the morning mist. Return to me, for I have redeemed you.

REFRESHMENT

ACTS 3:19

Repent, then, and turn to God,
so that your sins may be wiped out,
that times of refreshing
may come from the Lord.

PSALM 68:9

You gave abundant showers, O God;
you refreshed your weary inheritance.

JEREMIAH 31:25

I will refresh the weary and satisfy the
faint.

MATTHEW 11:28

Come to me, all you who are weary and
burdened, and I will give you rest.

PSALM 68:19

Praise be to the Lord, to God our Savior,
who daily bears our burdens.

Psalm 18:16

He reached down from on high
and took hold of me;
he drew me out of deep waters.

Psalm 107:6

They cried out to the LORD
in their trouble, and he delivered them
from their distress.

Revelation 21:4

He will wipe every tear from their eyes.
There will be no more death or mourning or crying or pain, for the old order
of things has passed away.

Psalm 116:8

For you, O LORD, have delivered my
soul from death, my eyes from tears,
my feet from stumbling.

Philemon 1:20

I do wish, brother, that I may have
some benefit from you in the Lord;
refresh my heart in Christ.

REPENTANCE

ACTS 2:38

Peter replied,
"Repent and be baptized,
every one of you,
in the name of Jesus Christ
for the forgiveness of your sins.
And you will receive
the gift of the Holy Spirit."

ACTS 3:19

Repent, then, and turn to God,
so that your sins may be wiped out,
that times of refreshing
may come from the Lord.

ROMANS 2:4

Do you show contempt
for the riches of his kindness,
tolerance and patience,
not realizing that God's kindness
leads you toward repentance?

Isaiah 30:15

This is what the Sovereign LORD,
the Holy One of Israel, says:
"In repentance and rest
is your salvation,
in quietness and trust
is your strength,
but you would have none of it."

2 Peter 3:9

The Lord is not slow
in keeping his promise,
as some understand slowness.
He is patient with you,
not wanting anyone to perish,
but everyone to come to repentance.

Luke 15:7

I tell you that in the same way
there will be more rejoicing in heaven
over one sinner who repents
than over ninety-nine righteous persons
who do not need to repent.

2 CORINTHIANS 7:10

Godly sorrow brings repentance
that leads to salvation
and leaves no regret,
but worldly sorrow brings death.

2 CHRONICLES 7:14

If my people,
who are called by my name,
will humble themselves and pray
and seek my face
and turn from their wicked ways,
then will I hear from heaven
and will forgive their sin
and will heal their land.

EZEKIEL 18:21

If a wicked man turns away from
all the sins he has committed
and keeps all my decrees
and does what is just and right,
he will surely live;
he will not die.

ISAIAH 55:7

Let the wicked forsake his way
and the evil man his thoughts.
Let him turn to the LORD,
and he will have mercy on him,
and to our God,
for he will freely pardon.

LUKE 5:31-32

Jesus answered them,
"It is not the healthy who need a doctor,
but the sick.
I have not come to call the righteous,
but sinners to repentance."

LUKE 15:10

In the same way,
I tell you, there is rejoicing
in the presence of the angels of God
over one sinner who repents.

REST

JEREMIAH 6:16

This is what the LORD says:
"Stand at the crossroads and look;
ask for the ancient paths,
ask where the good way is, and walk in it,
and you will find rest for your souls."

PSALM 91:1

He who dwells in the shelter
of the Most High
will rest in the shadow of the Almighty.

MATTHEW 11:28-30

Come to me, all you who are weary
and burdened, and I will give you rest.
Take my yoke upon you and learn from me,
for I am gentle and humble in heart,
and you will find rest for your souls.
For my yoke is easy and my burden is light.

JEREMIAH 31:25

I will refresh the weary
and satisfy the faint.

PSALM 4:8

I will lie down and sleep in peace,
for you alone, O LORD,
make me dwell in safety.

PSALM 62:1–2

My soul finds rest in God alone;
my salvation comes from him.
He alone is my rock and my salvation;
he is my fortress, I will never be shaken.

EXODUS 33:14

The LORD replied, "My Presence will
go with you, and I will give you rest."

ISAIAH 32:18

My people will live in peaceful
dwelling places, in secure homes,
in undisturbed places of rest.

HEBREWS 4:9

There remains, then,
a Sabbath-rest for the people of God.

RESTORATION

PSALM 71:20–21

Though you have made me see troubles,
many and bitter, you will restore my
life again; from the depths of the earth
you will again bring me up.
You will increase my honor
and comfort me once again.

EZEKIEL 34:16

I will search for the lost and bring back
the strays. I will bind up the injured
and strengthen the weak, but the sleek
and the strong I will destroy.
I will shepherd the flock with justice.

JEREMIAH 30:17

"I will restore you to health and heal
your wounds," declares the LORD.

PSALM 80:3

Restore us, O God; make your face
shine upon us, that we may be saved.

ISAIAH 43:18–19

Forget the former things; do not dwell
on the past. See, I am doing a new thing!
Now it springs up; do you not perceive it?
I am making a way in the desert
and streams in the wasteland.

2 CORINTHIANS 5:17–18

If anyone is in Christ, he is a new creation; the old has gone, the new has come!
All this is from God, who reconciled us to
himself through Christ and gave us
the ministry of reconciliation.

1 PETER 5:10

The God of all grace, who called you to
his eternal glory in Christ, after you
have suffered a little while, will
himself restore you and make you
strong, firm and steadfast.

Reward

Jeremiah 17:10
I the LORD search the heart
and examine the mind,
to reward a man according to his conduct,
according to what his deeds deserve.

Revelation 22:12
Behold, I am coming soon!
My reward is with me,
and I will give to everyone
according to what he has done.

James 1:12
Blessed is the man
who perseveres under trial,
because when he has stood the test,
he will receive the crown of life that
God has promised to those who love him.

COLOSSIANS 3:23-24

Whatever you do, work at it with all
your heart, as working for the Lord,
not for men, since you know that you
will receive an inheritance
from the Lord as a reward.
It is the Lord Christ you are serving.

EPHESIANS 6:8

You know that the Lord will reward
everyone for whatever good he does,
whether he is slave or free.

MATTHEW 10:42

If anyone gives even a cup of cold water
to one of these little ones because he is
my disciple, I tell you the truth,
he will certainly not lose his reward.

LUKE 6:35

Love your enemies, do good to them,
and lend to them without
expecting to get anything back.
Then your reward will be great,
and you will be sons of the Most High,
because he is kind
to the ungrateful and wicked.

RIGHTEOUSNESS

MATTHEW 5:6

Blessed are those who hunger and
thirst for righteousness,
for they will be filled.

ISAIAH 32:17

The fruit of righteousness
will be peace;
the effect of righteousness will be
quietness and confidence forever.

PROVERBS 2:7-8

He holds victory in store for the upright,
he is a shield to those
whose walk is blameless,
for he guards the course of the just
and protects the way of his faithful ones.

PROVERBS 21:21

He who pursues righteousness and love
finds life, prosperity and honor.

PSALM 112:6-7

Surely he will never be shaken;
a righteous man will be
remembered forever. He will have no
fear of bad news; his heart is steadfast, trusting in the LORD.

PSALM 37:30-31

The mouth of the righteous man utters
wisdom, and his tongue speaks what is
just.
The law of his God is in his heart;
his feet do not slip.

JAMES 2:8

If you really keep the royal law
found in Scripture,
"Love your neighbor as yourself,"
you are doing right.

JAMES 1:27

Religion that God our Father accepts
as pure and faultless is this:
to look after orphans and widows
in their distress and to keep oneself
from being polluted by the world.

RIGHTEOUSNESS *of* GOD

PSALM 145:17
The LORD is righteous in all his ways
and loving toward all he has made.

PSALM 119:137
Righteous are you, O LORD,
and your laws are right.

JEREMIAH 23:5
"The days are coming,"
declares the LORD, "when I will raise up
to David a righteous Branch,
a king who will reign wisely
and do what is just and right in the land."

REVELATION 19:11
I saw heaven standing open and there
before me was a white horse,
whose rider is called Faithful and True.
With justice he judges and makes war.

2 CORINTHIANS 5:21

God made him who had no sin
to be sin for us, so that in him we might
become the righteousness of God.

1 JOHN 2:1-2

My dear children, I write this to you
so that you will not sin.
But if anybody does sin, we have one who
speaks to the Father in our defense—
Jesus Christ, the Righteous One.
He is the atoning sacrifice for our sins,
and not only for ours
but also for the sins of the whole world.

ROMANS 3:22

This righteousness from God comes through
faith in Jesus Christ to all who believe.

ROMANS 5:17

For if, by the trespass of the one man,
death reigned through that one man, how
much more will those who receive God's
abundant provision of grace and of the
gift of righteousness reign in life
through the one man, Jesus Christ.

SALVATION

1 TIMOTHY 2:3-4

God our Savior...
wants all men to be saved
and to come to a knowledge of the truth.

2 CORINTHIANS 6:2

For he says,
"In the time of my favor
I heard you,
and in the day of salvation
I helped you."
I tell you, now is the time of God's favor,
now is the day of salvation.

ROMANS 10:9

If you confess with your mouth,
"Jesus is Lord," and believe
in your heart that God raised him
from the dead, you will be saved.

ACTS 10:43

All the prophets testify about him that
everyone who believes in him receives
forgiveness of sins through his name.

HEBREWS 5:9

Once made perfect,
he became the source of
eternal salvation for all who obey him.

MARK 16:16

Whoever believes and is baptized
will be saved, but whoever does not
believe will be condemned.

TITUS 3:5

He saved us, not because
of righteous things we had done,
but because of his mercy.
He saved us through the washing of
rebirth and renewal by the Holy Spirit.

PSALM 40:2

He lifted me out of the slimy pit,
out of the mud and mire;
he set my feet on a rock
and gave me a firm place to stand.

SATISFACTION

ECCLESIASTES 2:24

A man can do nothing better
than to eat and drink and find
satisfaction in his work.
This too, I see, is from the hand of God.

PSALM 103:5

[The LORD] satisfies your desires with
good things so that your youth
is renewed like the eagle's.

PSALM 132:15

I will bless her with abundant provisions;
her poor will I satisfy with food.

PSALM 37:4

Delight yourself in the LORD and he will
give you the desires of your heart.

PSALM 107:8-9

Let them give thanks to the LORD
for his unfailing love
and his wonderful deeds for men,
for he satisfies the thirsty
and fills the hungry with good things.

PSALM 90:14

Satisfy us in the morning with your
unfailing love, that we may sing for joy
and be glad all our days.

JEREMIAH 31:25

I will refresh the weary
and satisfy the faint.

LUKE 6:21

Blessed are you who hunger now,
for you will be satisfied.
Blessed are you who weep now,
for you will laugh.

PSALM 91:16

With long life will I satisfy him
and show him my salvation.

SCRIPTURE

DEUTERONOMY 7:12

If you pay attention to these laws
and are careful to follow them,
then the LORD your God
will keep his covenant of love with you,
as he swore to your fore-fathers.

PSALM 19:7

The law of the LORD is perfect,
reviving the soul.
The statutes of the LORD are trustworthy,
making wise the simple.

ROMANS 15:4

For everything that was written in the past
was written to teach us, so that through
endurance and the encouragement of the
Scriptures we might have hope.

HEBREWS 4:12

For the word of God is living and active.
Sharper than any double-edged sword,
it penetrates even to dividing soul and
spirit, joints and marrow; it judges the
thoughts and attitudes of the heart.

2 TIMOTHY 3:16-17

All Scripture is God-breathed and is
useful for teaching, rebuking, correcting
and training in righteousness,
so that the man of God may be thoroughly
equipped for every good work.

JOSHUA 1:8

Do not let this Book of the Law depart
from your mouth; meditate on it day and
night, so that you may be careful
to do everything written in it.
Then you will be prosperous and successful.

MATTHEW 4:4

Jesus answered, "It is written: 'Man does
not live on bread alone, but on every word
that comes from the mouth of God.'"

SECURITY

PSALM 16:5

LORD, you have assigned me
my portion and my cup;
you have made my lot secure.

JEREMIAH 33:6

I will heal my people and will let them
enjoy abundant peace and security.

JOHN 10:28

I give them eternal life,
and they shall never perish;
no one can snatch them out of my hand.

PSALM 125:1

Those who trust in the LORD are like
Mount Zion, which cannot be shaken
but endures forever.

PSALM 16:8

I have set the LORD always before me.
Because he is at my right hand,
I will not be shaken.

PSALM 55:22

Cast your cares on the LORD
and he will sustain you;
he will never let the righteous fall.

HEBREWS 13:6

We say with confidence,
"The Lord is my helper; I will not
be afraid. What can man do to me?"

ROMANS 8:38-39

For I am convinced that neither death
nor life, neither angels nor demons,
neither the present nor the future,
nor any powers, neither height nor depth,
nor anything else in all creation,
will be able to separate us from the love
of God that is in Christ Jesus our Lord.

SELF-CONTROL

TITUS 2:11-12

For the grace of God that brings
salvation has appeared to all men.
It teaches us to say "No" to ungodliness
and worldly passions,
and to live self-controlled, upright
and godly lives in this present age.

1 PETER 1:13

Prepare your minds for action;
be self-controlled; set your hope fully
on the grace to be given you
when Jesus Christ is revealed.

1 PETER 4:7

The end of all things is near.
Therefore be clear minded
and self-controlled so that you can pray.

TITUS 2:2

Teach the older men to be temperate,
worthy of respect, self-controlled,
and sound in faith, in love
and in endurance.

MATTHEW 26:41

Watch and pray so that you
will not fall into temptation.
The spirit is willing, but the body is weak.

1 PETER 5:8

Be self-controlled and alert.
Your enemy the devil prowls around
like a roaring lion
looking for someone to devour.

ROMANS 8:13

For if you live according to the sinful
nature, you will die;
but if by the Spirit you put to death
the misdeeds of the body, you will live.

SELF-WORTH

JEREMIAH 31:3

The LORD appeared to us in the past, saying:
"I have loved you with an everlasting love;
I have drawn you with loving-kindness."

MATTHEW 10:29-31

Are not two sparrows sold for a penny?
Yet not one of them will fall to the ground
apart from the will of your Father.
And even the very hairs of your head
are all numbered. So don't be afraid;
you are worth more than many sparrows.

PSALM 100:3

Know that the LORD is God.
It is he who made us, and we are his;
we are his people, the sheep of his pasture.

PSALM 139:13-14

For you created my inmost being;
you knit me together in my mother's womb.
I praise you because I am fearfully and
wonderfully made;
your works are wonderful,
I know that full well.

ISAIAH 49:15-16

Can a mother forget the baby at her breast
and have no compassion
on the child she has borne?
Though she may forget,
I will not forget you!
See, I have engraved you on the palms of
my hands; your walls are ever before me.

EPHESIANS 1:5-6

He predestined us to be adopted as his
sons through Jesus Christ, in accordance
with his pleasure and will—to the praise
of his glorious grace, which he
has freely given us in the One he loves.

SERENITY

PSALM 46:10

Be still, and know that I am God;
I will be exalted among the nations,
I will be exalted in the earth.

PSALM 4:4

In your anger do not sin;
when you are on your beds,
search your hearts and be silent.

PSALM 89:9

You rule over the surging sea;
when its waves mount up, you still them.

PSALM 107:28-30

Then they cried out to the LORD
in their trouble, and he brought them
out of their distress. He stilled the storm
to a whisper; the waves of the sea were
hushed. They were glad when it grew calm,
and he guided them to their desired haven.

Psalm 4:8

I will lie down and sleep in peace,
for you alone, O LORD,
make me dwell in safety.

Psalm 23:1-2

The LORD is my shepherd,
I shall not be in want.
He makes me lie down in green pastures,
he leads me beside quiet waters.

1 Corinthians 14:33

For God is not a God of disorder
but of peace.

Proverbs 1:33

Whoever listens to me will live in safety
and be at ease, without fear of harm.

1 Thessalonians 4:11-12

Make it your ambition to lead a quiet
life, to mind your own business and to
work with your hands, just as we told you,
so that your daily life may win the
respect of outsiders and so that you will
not be dependent on anybody.

SERVING

EPHESIANS 6:7
Serve wholeheartedly, as if you were
serving the Lord, not men.

1 CHRONICLES 28:9
Acknowledge the God of your father,
and serve him with wholehearted devotion
and with a willing mind, for the LORD
searches every heart and understands
every motive behind the thoughts.
If you seek him, he will be found by you;
but if you forsake him,
he will reject you forever.

COLOSSIANS 3:23-24
Whatever you do, work at it with all your
heart, as working for the Lord, not for
men, since you know that you will receive
an inheritance from the Lord as a reward.
It is the Lord Christ you are serving.

ROMANS 12:11

Keep your spiritual fervor,
serving the Lord.

1 PETER 4:11

If anyone speaks, he should do it as one
speaking the very words of God.
If anyone serves, he should do it with the
strength God provides, so that in all
things God may be praised through Jesus
Christ. To him be the glory and the power
for ever and ever. Amen.

JAMES 2:15-16

Suppose a brother or sister is without
clothes and daily food. If one of you says
to him, "Go, I wish you well; keep warm
and well fed," but does nothing about his
physical needs, what good is it?

JAMES 1:27

Religion that God our Father accepts
as pure and faultless is this:
to look after orphans and widows
in their distress and to keep oneself
from being polluted by the world.

SINCERITY

1 TIMOTHY 1:5

The goal of this command is love,
which comes from a pure heart and
a good conscience and a sincere faith.

1 JOHN 3:18

Dear children, let us not love with words
or tongue but with actions and in truth.

JAMES 2:14, 18

What good is it, my brothers, if a man
claims to have faith but has no deeds?
Can such faith save him?
But someone will say,
"You have faith; I have deeds."
Show me your faith without deeds,
and I will show you my faith by what I do.

JOSHUA 24:14

Now fear the LORD and serve him with
all faithfulness.

Philippians 1:9-10

This is my prayer: that your love may abound more and more in knowledge and depth of insight, so that you may be able to discern what is best and may be pure and blameless until the day of Christ.

Hebrews 10:19, 22

Brothers, since we have confidence to enter the Most Holy Place by the blood of Jesus, ...let us draw near to God with a sincere heart in full assurance of faith, having our hearts sprinkled to cleanse us from a guilty conscience and having our bodies washed with pure water.

2 Corinthians 1:12

Now this is our boast: Our conscience testifies that we have conducted ourselves in the world, and especially in our relations with you, in the holiness and sincerity that are from God. We have done so not according to worldly wisdom but according to God's grace.

SINGLENESS

PSALM 68:6

God sets the lonely in families,
he leads forth the prisoners with singing;
but the rebellious
live in a sun-scorched land.

MATTHEW 28:20

Surely I am with you always,
to the very end of the age.

PSALM 73:23

Yet I am always with you;
you hold me by my right hand.

HOSEA 2:19-20

I will betroth you to me forever;
I will betroth you in righteousness
and justice, in love and compassion.
I will betroth you in faithfulness,
and you will acknowledge the LORD.

ISAIAH 61:10

I delight greatly in the LORD;
my soul rejoices in my God.
For he has clothed me with garments
of salvation and arrayed me in a robe of
righteousness, as a bridegroom adorns
his head like a priest, and as a bride
adorns herself with her jewels.

ISAIAH 54:5

For your Maker is your husband—
the LORD Almighty is his name—
the Holy One of Israel is your Redeemer;
he is called the God of all the earth.

1 CORINTHIANS 7:32

I would like you to be free from concern.
An unmarried man is concerned
about the Lord's affairs—
how he can please the Lord.

1 CORINTHIANS 7:34

An unmarried woman or virgin
is concerned about the Lord's affairs:
Her aim is to be devoted to the Lord
in both body and spirit.

SPEECH

PROVERBS 21:23
He who guards his mouth and his tongue
keeps himself from calamity.

ECCLESIASTES 9:17
The quiet words of the wise
are more to be heeded
than the shouts of a ruler of fools.

EPHESIANS 4:29
Do not let any unwholesome talk come out
of your mouths, but only what is helpful
for building others up according to their
needs, that it may benefit those who listen.

PROVERBS 15:1
A gentle answer turns away wrath.

1 PETER 4:11

If anyone speaks, he should do it as one
speaking the very words of God.
If anyone serves, he should do it with the
strength God provides, so that in all
things God may be praised
through Jesus Christ. To him be the glory
and the power for ever and ever. Amen.

PROVERBS 15:4

The tongue that brings healing
is a tree of life,
but a deceitful tongue crushes the spirit.

EPHESIANS 4:15

Speaking the truth in love,
we will in all things grow up into him
who is the Head, that is, Christ.

PROVERBS 16:24

Pleasant words are a honeycomb,
sweet to the soul and healing to the bones.

PROVERBS 25:11

A word aptly spoken is like apples of gold
in settings of silver.

STABILITY

PSALM 16:8

I have set the LORD always before me.
Because he is at my right hand,
I will not be shaken.

ISAIAH 54:10

"Though the mountains be shaken
and the hills be removed,
yet my unfailing love for you
will not be shaken nor my covenant of
peace be removed," says the LORD,
who has compassion on you.

PSALM 62:1–2

My soul finds rest in God alone;
my salvation comes from him.
He alone is my rock and my salvation;
he is my fortress, I will never be shaken.

PSALM 40:1-2

I waited patiently for the LORD;
he turned to me and heard my cry.
He lifted me out of the slimy pit,
out of the mud and mire; he set my feet on
a rock and gave me a firm place to stand.

JUDE 1:24-25

To him who is able to keep you from
falling and to present you before his
glorious presence without fault and with
great joy—to the only God our Savior
be glory, majesty, power and authority,
through Jesus Christ our Lord, before all
ages, now and forevermore! Amen.

PSALM 119:165

Great peace have they who love your law,
and nothing can make them stumble.

PSALM 37:23-24

If the LORD delights in a man's way,
he makes his steps firm;
though he stumble, he will not fall,
for the LORD upholds him with his hand.

STRENGTH

ISAIAH 41:10

So do not fear,
for I am with you;
do not be dismayed,
for I am your God.
I will strengthen you and help you;
I will uphold you
with my righteous right hand.

PHILIPPIANS 4:13

I can do everything through him
who gives me strength.

PSALM 73:26

My flesh and my heart may fail,
but God is the strength of my heart
and my portion forever.

ISAIAH 40:29

He gives strength to the weary
and increases the power of the weak.

2 Corinthians 12:9

He said to me,
"My grace is sufficient for you,
for my power is made perfect
in weakness."
Therefore I will boast all the more
gladly about my weaknesses,
so that Christ's power
may rest on me.

2 Samuel 22:33–34

It is God who arms me
with strength and makes my way perfect.
He makes my feet
like the feet of a deer;
he enables me to stand on the heights.

Ezekiel 34:16

I will search for the lost
and bring back the strays.
I will bind up the injured
and strengthen the weak,
but the sleek and the strong
I will destroy. I will shepherd the flock
with justice.

Psalm 29:11

The LORD gives strength to his people;
the LORD blesses his people with peace.

Exodus 15:2

The LORD is my strength and my song;
he has become my salvation.
He is my God, and I will praise him,
my father's God, and I will exalt him.

Psalm 59:16

I will sing of your strength,
in the morning I will sing of your love;
for you are my fortress,
my refuge in times of trouble.

1 Thessalonians 3:13

May he strengthen your hearts
so that you will be blameless
and holy in the presence of our God
and Father when our Lord Jesus
comes with all his holy ones.

Psalm 46:1

God is our refuge and strength,
an ever-present help in trouble.

ISAIAH 40:27-31

Why do you say, O Jacob,
and complain, O Israel,
"My way is hidden from the Lord;
my cause is disregarded by my God"?
Do you not know?
Have you not heard?
The LORD is the everlasting God,
the Creator of the ends of the earth.
He will not grow tired or weary,
and his understanding no one can fathom.
He gives strength to the weary
and increases the power of the weak.
Even youths grow tired and weary,
and young men stumble and fall;
but those who hope in the LORD
will renew their strength.
They will soar on wings like eagles;
they will run and not grow weary,
they will walk and not be faint.

SUCCESS

DEUTERONOMY 29:9

Carefully follow the terms of this
covenant, so that you may prosper
in everything you do.

1 CHRONICLES 22:13

Then you will have success if
you are careful to observe
the decrees and laws that
the LORD gave Moses for Israel.
Be strong and courageous.
Do not be afraid or discouraged.

JOSHUA 1:7

Be strong and very courageous.
Be careful to obey all the law
my servant Moses gave you;
do not turn from it to the right
or to the left, that you may be
successful wherever you go.

Psalm 1:2-3

His delight is in
the law of the LORD, and on his law
he meditates day and night.
He is like a tree
planted by streams of water,
which yields its fruit in season
and whose leaf does not wither.
Whatever he does prospers.

Psalm 20:4

May he give you the desire of your heart
and make all your plans succeed.

Proverbs 15:22

Plans fail for lack of counsel,
but with many advisers they succeed.

Proverbs 16:3

Commit to the LORD whatever you do,
and your plans will succeed.

Zechariah 4:6

"Not by might nor by power,
but by my Spirit,"
says the LORD Almighty.

THANKFULNESS

COLOSSIANS 3:16
Let the word of Christ dwell in you
richly as you teach and admonish one
another with all wisdom, and as you
sing psalms, hymns and spiritual songs
with gratitude in your hearts to God.

COLOSSIANS 2:6-7
So then, just as you received
Christ Jesus as Lord,
continue to live in him, rooted
and built up in him, strengthened
in the faith as you were taught, and
overflowing with thankfulness.

PSALM 107:8-9
Let them give thanks to the LORD for his
unfailing love and his wonderful deeds
for men, for he satisfies the thirsty and
fills the hungry with good things.

Psalm 30:11–12

You turned my wailing into dancing; you removed my sackcloth and clothed me with joy, that my heart may sing to you and not be silent. O LORD my God, I will give you thanks forever.

1 Chronicles 16:34

Give thanks to the LORD, for he is good; his love endures forever.

Psalm 28:7

The LORD is my strength and my shield; my heart trusts in him, and I am helped. My heart leaps for joy and I will give thanks to him in song.

Hebrews 12:28

Since we are receiving a kingdom that cannot be shaken, let us be thankful, and so worship God acceptably with reverence and awe.

1 Thessalonians 5:18

Give thanks in all circumstances, for this is God's will for you in Christ Jesus.

THOUGHTS

PHILIPPIANS 4:8
Finally, brothers, whatever is true,
whatever is noble, whatever is right,
whatever is pure, whatever is lovely,
whatever is admirable—
if anything is excellent or praiseworthy—
think about such things.

ROMANS 12:2
Be transformed
by the renewing of your mind.
Then you will be able to test and
approve what God's will is—
his good, pleasing and perfect will.

2 CORINTHIANS 10:5
We demolish arguments and
every pretension that sets itself up
against the knowledge of God,
and we take captive every thought
to make it obedient to Christ.

Romans 8:6

The mind controlled by the Spirit
is life and peace.

Proverbs 12:5

The plans of the righteous are just,
but the advice of the wicked is deceitful.

Psalm 94:11

The LORD knows the thoughts of man;
he knows that they are futile.

Isaiah 26:3

You will keep in perfect peace
him whose mind is steadfast,
because he trusts in you.

Jeremiah 17:10

"I the LORD search the heart
and examine the mind,
to reward a man according to his conduct,
according to what his deeds deserve."

Matthew 5:8

Blessed are the pure in heart,
for they will see God.

TRUST

PSALM 40:4

Blessed is the man
who makes the LORD his trust,
who does not look to the proud,
to those who turn aside to false gods.

ISAIAH 30:15

This is what the Sovereign LORD, the
Holy One of Israel, says:
"In repentance and rest is your salvation,
in quietness and trust is your strength."

ISAIAH 28:16

So this is what the Sovereign LORD says:
"See, I lay a stone in Zion,
a tested stone, a precious cornerstone
for a sure foundation;
the one who trusts
will never be dismayed."

Psalm 118:8

It is better to take refuge in the LORD
than to trust in man.

John 14:1

Trust in God; trust also in me.

Isaiah 26:3–4

You will keep in perfect peace
him whose mind is steadfast,
because he trusts in you.
Trust in the LORD forever,
for the LORD, the LORD,
is the Rock eternal.

Jeremiah 17:7–8

Blessed is the man
who trusts in the LORD,
whose confidence is in him.
He will be like a tree
planted by the water that sends out
its roots by the stream.
It does not fear when heat comes;
its leaves are always green.
It has no worries in a year of drought
and never fails to bear fruit.

TRUTH

PROVERBS 16:13
Kings take pleasure in honest lips;
they value a man who speaks the truth.

PSALM 145:18
The LORD is near to all who call on him,
to all who call on him in truth.

JOHN 14:6
Jesus answered,
"I am the way and the truth and the life.
No one comes to the Father
except through me."

JOHN 8:32
You will know the truth,
and the truth will set you free.

PSALM 119:160
All your words are true;
all your righteous laws are eternal.

1 JOHN 5:20

We know also that the Son of God has
come and has given us understanding,
so that we may know him who is true.
And we are in him who is true—
even in his Son Jesus Christ.
He is the true God and eternal life.

JOHN 16:13

When he, the Spirit of truth, comes,
he will guide you into all truth.
He will not speak on his own;
he will speak only what he hears,
and he will tell you what is yet to come.

PROVERBS 23:23

Buy the truth and do not sell it;
get wisdom, discipline and understanding.

JOSHUA 23:14

Now I am about to go the way
of all the earth. You know with all your
heart and soul that not one of all the
good promises the LORD your God gave
you has failed. Every promise has been
fulfilled; not one has failed.

UNITY

How good and pleasant it is
when brothers live together in unity!

There is one body and one Spirit—
one Lord, one faith, one baptism;
one God and Father of all, who is over
all and through all and in all.

There is neither Jew nor Greek,
slave nor free, male nor female,
for you are all one in Christ Jesus.

Brothers, good-by.
Aim for perfection, listen to my appeal,
be of one mind, live in peace.
And the God of love
and peace will be with you.

COLOSSIANS 2:2

My purpose is that they may be
encouraged in heart and united in love,
so that they may have the full riches
of complete understanding, in order
that they may know the mystery of God,
namely, Christ.

1 CORINTHIANS 12:13

For we were all baptized by one Spirit
into one body—whether Jews or
Greeks, slave or free—and we were all
given the one Spirit to drink.

EPHESIANS 4:11-13

It was he who gave some to be apostles,
some to be prophets, some to be
evangelists, and some to be pastors and
teachers, to prepare God's people
for works of service, so that the body
of Christ may be built up until
we all reach unity in the faith
and in the knowledge of the Son of God
and become mature,
attaining to the whole measure
of the fullness of Christ.

VICTORY

1 CORINTHIANS 15:57

Thanks be to God! He gives us the
victory through our Lord Jesus Christ.

JOHN 16:33

I have told you these things,
so that in me you may have peace.
In this world you will have trouble.
But take heart! I have overcome the world.

1 JOHN 5:4-5

For everyone born of God overcomes
the world. This is the victory that has
overcome the world, even our faith.
Who is it that overcomes the world?
Only he who believes
that Jesus is the Son of God.

PSALM 60:12

With God we will gain the victory,
and he will trample down our enemies.

ROMANS 16:20

The God of peace
will soon crush Satan under your feet.
The grace of our Lord Jesus be with you.

1 JOHN 4:4

You, dear children, are from God
and have overcome them,
because the one who is in you is greater
than the one who is in the world.

ROMANS 8:37

In all these things we are more than
conquerors through him who loved us.

1 CORINTHIANS 15:54

When the perishable has been clothed
with the imperishable, and the mortal
with immortality, then the saying that is
written will come true:
"Death has been swallowed up in victory."

PROVERBS 2:7

He holds victory in store
for the upright, he is a shield to those
whose walk is blameless.

WEALTH

PROVERBS 22:2

Rich and poor have this in common:
The LORD is the Maker of them all.

JAMES 2:5

Listen, my dear brothers:
Has not God chosen those who are poor
in the eyes of the world to be rich in
faith and to inherit the kingdom he
promised those who love him?

DEUTERONOMY 8:18

Remember the LORD your God,
for it is he who gives you the ability
to produce wealth, and so confirms
his covenant, which he swore to your
forefathers, as it is today.

PROVERBS 11:4

Wealth is worthless in the day of wrath.

1 TIMOTHY 6:17-19

Command those who are rich in this
present world not to be arrogant nor
to put their hope in wealth,
which is so uncertain, but to put their
hope in God, who richly provides us
with everything for our enjoyment.
Command them to do good,
to be rich in good deeds, and to be generous
and willing to share. In this way
they will lay up treasure for themselves
as a firm foundation for the coming age,
so that they may take hold of the life
that is truly life.

1 TIMOTHY 6:7

For we brought nothing into the world,
and we can take nothing out of it.

PROVERBS 3:9-10

Honor the LORD with your wealth,
with the firstfruits of all your crops;
then your barns will be filled
to overflowing, and your vats
will brim over with new wine.

WILL *of* GOD

Be joyful always; pray continually;
give thanks in all circumstances,
for this is God's will for you
in Christ Jesus.

ROMANS 12:2
Be transformed by the renewing of
your mind. Then you will be able to test
and approve what God's will is—his
good, pleasing and perfect will.

GALATIANS 1:3–5
Grace and peace to you from God our
Father and the Lord Jesus Christ,
who gave himself for our sins to rescue us
from the present evil age, according to
the will of our God and Father,
to whom be glory for ever and ever. Amen.

Ephesians 1:9-10

He made known to us the mystery of his
will according to his good pleasure,
which he purposed in Christ,
to be put into effect when the times will
have reached their fulfillment—
to bring all things in heaven and on earth
together under one head, even Christ.

1 John 2:17

The world and its desires pass away,
but the man who does the will of God
lives forever.

John 6:40

For my Father's will is that everyone who
looks to the Son and believes in him
shall have eternal life, and I will raise
him up at the last day.

1 Thessalonians 4:3-4

It is God's will that you should
be sanctified: that you should avoid sexual
immorality; that each of you
should learn to control his own body
in a way that is holy and honorable.

WISDOM

PSALM 111:10

The fear of the LORD is the beginning
of wisdom; all who follow his precepts
have good understanding.
To him belongs eternal praise.

1 CORINTHIANS 1:25

For the foolishness of God is wiser
than man's wisdom, and the weakness
of God is stronger than man's strength.

JAMES 1:5

If any of you lacks wisdom,
he should ask God, who gives generously
to all without finding fault,
and it will be given to him.

PROVERBS 4:7

Wisdom is supreme;
therefore get wisdom. Though it cost all
you have, get understanding.

PROVERBS 24:14

Know also that wisdom is sweet
to your soul; if you find it,
there is a future hope for you,
and your hope will not be cut off.

ECCLESIASTES 7:11–12

Wisdom, like an inheritance,
is a good thing and benefits those
who see the sun. Wisdom is a shelter
as money is a shelter, but the advantage
of knowledge is this: that wisdom
preserves the life of its possessor.

PROVERBS 16:16

How much better to get wisdom than gold,
to choose understanding rather than silver!

ECCLESIASTES 7:19

Wisdom makes one wise man more powerful
than ten rulers in a city.

JAMES 3:17

The wisdom that comes from heaven is
first of all pure; then peace-loving,
considerate, submissive, full of mercy
and good fruit, impartial and sincere.

WITNESSING

ISAIAH 52:7

How beautiful on the mountains
are the feet of those who bring good news,
who proclaim peace, who bring
good tidings, who proclaim salvation,
who say to Zion, "Your God reigns!"

MATTHEW 28:18-20

Then Jesus came to them and said,
"All authority in heaven and on earth
has been given to me. Therefore go
and make disciples of all nations,
baptizing them in the name of the Father
and of the Son and of the Holy Spirit,
and teaching them to obey everything
I have commanded you.
And surely I am with you always,
to the very end of the age."

2 CORINTHIANS 4:13

It is written: "I believed; therefore
I have spoken." With that same spirit of
faith we also believe and therefore speak.

MARK 16:15

He said to them, "Go into all the world
and preach the good news to all creation."

1 PETER 3:15-16

Do this with gentleness and respect,
keeping a clear conscience, so that those
who speak maliciously against
your good behavior in Christ may be
ashamed of their slander.

MATTHEW 5:16

In the same way, let your light shine
before men, that they may see your good
deeds and praise your Father in heaven.

MATTHEW 24:14

This gospel of the kingdom will be
preached in the whole world
as a testimony to all nations,
and then the end will come.

WIVES

PROVERBS 18:22

He who finds a wife finds what is good
and receives favor from the LORD.

PROVERBS 19:14

Houses and wealth
are inherited from parents,
but a prudent wife is from the LORD.

SONG OF SONGS 4:9–10

You have stolen my heart, my sister,
my bride; you have stolen my heart
with one glance of your eyes,
with one jewel of your necklace.
How delightful is your love,
my sister, my bride!
How much more pleasing is your love
than wine, and the fragrance of your
perfume than any spice!

PROVERBS 31:10

A wife of noble character who can find?
She is worth far more than rubies.

1 CORINTHIANS 7:4

The wife's body does not belong to her
alone but also to her husband.
In the same way, the husband's body
does not belong to him alone
but also to his wife.

EPHESIANS 5:22-23

Wives, submit to your husbands
as to the Lord. For the husband
is the head of the wife as Christ
is the head of the church,
his body, of which he is the Savior.

PROVERBS 31:27-28

She watches over the affairs
of her household and
does not eat the bread of idleness.
Her children arise and call her blessed;
her husband also, and he praises her.

WOMEN

1 PETER 3:3-4
Your beauty should not come from
outward adornment, such as braided hair
and the wearing of gold jewelry
and fine clothes. Instead, it should be that
of your inner self, the unfading beauty of
a gentle and quiet spirit,
which is of great worth in God's sight.

PROVERBS 31:30
Charm is deceptive, and beauty is fleeting;
but a woman who fears the
LORD is to be praised.

PROVERBS 11:16
A kindhearted woman gains respect,
but ruthless men gain only wealth.

PROVERBS 31:20

She opens her arms to the poor
and extends her hands to the needy.

TITUS 2:3-5

Teach the older women to be reverent
in the way they live, not to be slanderers
or addicted to much wine, but to teach
what is good. Then they can train the
younger women to love their husbands
and children, to be self-controlled
and pure, to be busy at home, to be kind,
and to be subject to their husbands,
so that no one will malign the word of God.

PROVERBS 14:1

The wise woman builds her house,
but with her own hands
the foolish one tears hers down.

1 CORINTHIANS 11:3

Now I want you to realize that the head
of every man is Christ,
and the head of the woman is man,
and the head of Christ is God.

WORK

1 CORINTHIANS 15:58

My dear brothers, stand firm.
Let nothing move you.
Always give yourselves fully to the
work of the Lord, because you know
that your labor in the Lord is not in vain.

ROMANS 12:11

Never be lacking in zeal, but keep your
spiritual fervor, serving the Lord.

TITUS 3:14

Our people must learn to devote
themselves to doing what is good,
in order that they may provide for daily
necessities and not live unproductive lives.

ECCLESIASTES 5:18

I realized that it is good and proper
for a man to eat and drink, and to find
satisfaction in his toilsome labor
under the sun during the few days of life
God has given him.

PROVERBS 13:4

Diligent hands bring wealth.

PROVERBS 10:4

The desires of the diligent
are fully satisfied.

ECCLESIASTES 5:12

The sleep of a laborer is sweet,
whether he eats little or much,
but the abundance of a rich man
permits him no sleep.

HEBREWS 4:9-10

There remains, then, a Sabbath-rest
for the people of God;
for anyone who enters God's rest
also rests from his own work,
just as God did from his.

WORSHIP

PSALM 29:2

Ascribe to the LORD the glory
due his name; worship the LORD
in the splendor of his holiness.

PSALM 43:4

Then will I go to the altar of God,
to God, my joy and my delight.
I will praise you with the harp,
O God, my God.

EXODUS 15:1-2

I will sing to the LORD,
for he is highly exalted.
The horse and its rider
he has hurled into the sea.
The LORD is my strength and my song;
he has become my salvation.
He is my God, and I will praise him,
my father's God, and I will exalt him.

PSALM 95:6

Come, let us bow down in worship,
let us kneel before the LORD our Maker.

PSALM 100:2

Worship the LORD with gladness;
come before him with joyful songs.

HEBREWS 12:28

Since we are receiving a kingdom
that cannot be shaken,
let us be thankful, and so worship God
acceptably with reverence and awe.

ROMANS 12:1

I urge you, brothers,
in view of God's mercy,
to offer your bodies as living
sacrifices, holy and pleasing to God—
this is your spiritual act of worship. 1

1 CHRONICLES 16:25

Great is the LORD
and most worthy of praise;
he is to be feared above all gods.

MALACHI 4:2

For you who revere my name,
the sun of righteousness will rise
with healing in its wings.
And you will go out and leap like
calves released from the stall.

JOHN 4:23-24

A time is coming and has now come
when the true worshipers will worship
the Father in spirit and truth,
for they are the kind of worshipers
the Father seeks.
God is spirit, and his worshipers
must worship in spirit and in truth.

PSALM 81:1-3

Sing for joy to God our strength;
shout aloud to the God of Jacob!
Begin the music, strike the tambourine,
play the melodious harp and lyre.
Sound the ram's horn at the New Moon,
and when the moon is full,
on the day of our Feast;

"Praise be to the LORD,
who has given rest to his people Israel
just as he promised.
Not one word has failed
of all the good promises he gave
through his servant Moses.
May the LORD our God be with us
as he was with our fathers;
may he never leave us nor forsake us.
May he turn our hearts to him,
to walk in all his ways
and to keep the commands, decrees
and regulations he gave our fathers.
And may these words of mine,
which I have prayed before the LORD,
be near to the LORD our God
day and night, that he may uphold the
cause of his servant and the cause
of his people Israel according to
each day's need, so that all the peoples
of the earth may know that the LORD
is God and that there is no other.
But your hearts must be fully committed
to the LORD our God, to live by his
decrees and obey his commands,
as at this time."

INDEX

At Inspirio we love to hear from you—
your stories, your feedback,
and your product ideas.
Please send your comments to us
by way of e-mail at
icares@zondervan.com
or to the address below:

inspirio

Attn: Inspirio Cares
5300 Patterson Avenue SE
Grand Rapids, MI 49530

If you would like further information
about Inspirio and the products we
create, please visit us at:
www.inspiriogifts.com

Thank you and God bless!